THE SKILLS OF PLEASURE

Crafting the Life You Want

Stewart Blackburn

Hale Onaona Publishing
12-7002 Lahela St.
Pahoa, HI 96778

FIRST EDITION

Cover & interior design by Indie Author Services. Photography from Shutterstock, Inc.

ISBN-13: 978-1481800419
ISBN-10: 1481800418

Visit www.stewartblackburn.com for more information about the author.

Dedicated to all the pioneers and scouts in the realms of pleasure,
who seek to expand the boundaries of the known world of joy and bliss.

Acknowledgments

I am deeply grateful to the many people who contributed their time, effort, and inspiration to this book.

I would especially like to thank Dr. Serge Kahili King for your amazing teachings, your kind mentorship, and, most of all, your friendship.

A deep bow and thank you to Diane Koerner and Roger Harris for all the hard work you did in editing and supporting this work.

Thank you to Dr. Joseph Kramer for your inspired work in the world of erotic healing and trance, as well as, for all the personal discussions in the seminal development of this work.

Thank you to Harry Faddis for the Three-Minute Game.

Thank you to Syd, Soma and Solomon, Gail and Walter, Moisés, Lucy and John, Gary, Patricia and Mark, and Gloria for all your invaluable comments on this work.

And thank you to Pono, my Puna dog who slept through the whole process!

TABLE OF CONTENTS

INTRODUCTION

*"All animals, except man, know that the principal business of life
is to enjoy it."*

—Samuel Butler

This book is about looking at pleasure as a *much* more important
part of our lives than we give it credit for. There are significant
ways that we can work with pleasure, not just for enjoying life more,
but also to be more effective, creative, caring, loving, healthy, spiritually connected…and happy.

What does it take to feel really good? It seems like we should
know the answer to this, but few of us do. What is holding us back
from thoroughly enjoying our lives the way we want to? Even those of
us who read a lot of books on the subject and attend workshops find
our experience of joy to be fleeting and incomplete. Is there some way
we can hold onto the great feelings we occasionally get to experience?
The comings and goings of pleasure and joy seem as mysterious as the
favor of Lady Luck. Is there an upper limit to the joy we can experience? It appears so, although there doesn't seem to be any real reason
for it.

These are natural questions and answers that arise because we have never been taught the skills necessary for truly enjoying our existence. We have certainly been taught the skills of survival in our society, the ways that we need to work and behave in order to get along and live reasonable lives. But these are not the skills that take us to the great places we are capable of visiting. The skills that are presented here, skills that anyone can learn and practice, lead to an extraordinary life that has been hidden from most people. Some who have looked hard have found them. Others have stumbled upon them. But they are available to all. It just takes some effort. Each step, though, is rewarded with an increase of pleasure and every little bit of practice brings greater joy and happiness.

The Skills of Pleasure present a different way of looking at how we live. This approach looks at feelings as the primary focus of life and stresses the importance of taking personal responsibility for those feelings. The things that we say are the most important to us, things like love, compassion, harmony, peace, and joy, are all feelings. Underneath every desire for an object or experience is a desire for one or more feelings. And we have no better definition of health than simply feeling good.

Our world is changing both in obvious ways and in subtler, energetic ways, and now is the time to be very clear about how we want our world to look and function. The old ways of thinking and feeling aren't working well. The effects of those outdated modes of operating are glaringly spread around the world in pain and suffering. That's easy to see. But it doesn't have to be that way.

There is no reason why we can't live an exciting joyful life starting today. We will certainly have challenges in life and some things will undoubtedly happen that we don't like. But the key to happiness is in how we handle these things. With practice we can feel ever-increasing joy and love while being very grounded in this earthly plane. As we become happier we are able to help others better and the ripples of our joy can wash over the entire world.

Pleasure shapes everything we can think of. Our whole view of life is structured around how we think we can get the most pleasure. It is such a pervasive part of our lives that we seldom really even notice it. And yet it is what we crave and value the most.

We work for money so that we can buy things that will help us feel good, like a good place to live, good food for our table, and things and experiences that we can enjoy. We help others, when we can, because it feels good. The same is true of cleaning the house, taking care of chores, and paying bills. There is a pleasure in getting these things done and in enjoying the fruits of our efforts.

"Pleasure is Nature's test, her sign of approval. When man is happy, he is in harmony with himself and his environment."
—Oscar Wilde

You might not think it at first, but all religions are based on pleasure. Each one in its own way describes a life of greater pleasure at some point if we will only follow its precepts. That pleasure may not be immediate, but it is promised to come. In some religions we may have to wait until after we die. In others we may have to wait even longer. The immediate pleasure, though, is in enjoying the anticipation of how things will be later.

Some philosophers and scientists say that feelings originate in the body; others say that they originate in the mind. Both camps leave out that part of us that is beyond the physical body and the conscious mind. This is the transcendent experience that is often referred to as the Divine. We all have some experience of something that is "greater than ourselves."

Every culture makes references to these experiences and their explanations form at least part of the basis of that culture. Since these are such personal experiences it's no wonder that we have so many different names for them: God, ancestors, spirit guides, angels, the Buddha-within, Source, All-That-Is, Allah, Wakan-Tanka, Shiva, and Jesus to name only a few. For every name there is a story that helps us understand something about what we are experiencing. And each story in its own way colors the experience. But what is common is that there is something, either built into each of us or surrounding us, which is there to love and guide us, if we will only pay attention to it and ask for its help. I will simply refer to this experience as Higher Mind. Please substitute your own word or concept whenever you see my words for it, if you like. From my perspective, it doesn't matter what we call it.

> "What's in a name? That which we call a rose
> By any other name would smell as sweet."
> —William Shakespeare

Not taking that transcendent part into account is like describing how a car works without ever mentioning gasoline. Simply put, feeling good is the experience of being in harmony with our being, including our spirit, and feeling bad is the experience of being out of harmony. The greater the good feeling, the greater the connection and harmony is.

This experience of connection with Spirit, however that is conceived, is always described as an immense pleasure. Words like bliss, ecstasy, and immeasurable joy are used regularly. Things are sacred because they are important to us and, behind all the rationale and dogma, what is important is feeling good. People pray or meditate because it makes them feel good. Gathering with like-minded people, the joy of connection with others while sharing a vision of profound love is one of the most pleasurable experiences that many of us have on a regular basis.

The feelings of being loved, respected, valued, heard, desired, and safe are all vital pleasures. They are connected to our sense of who we are and without them we experience a sense of threat to our very survival. We go to great lengths to get others to inspire and evoke these feelings of self-love in us. Romantic relationships are built around these feelings and the mutual effort to keep these feelings alive.

> "Be happy. It's one way of being wise."
> —Colette

The potential for pleasure is everywhere. While we are all motivated by it and we can experience it at any time, lots of people don't feel much pleasure at all. That's such a shame. It seems that in many ways we have lost touch with the experience of true, deep, soul satisfying, deeply nurturing, and joyous pleasure. Whether it's because of stress or lack of understanding, we simply do not enjoy ourselves the way we could.

I believe that a big part of the issue here is that most of us don't really understand the nature of pleasure and how it works. We also don't appreciate the power of pleasure, how it influences our health, and how it is an important factor in bringing what we want into our lives. We also don't see how it works as a natural guidance system.

> *"Felicity, the companion of content, is rather found*
> *in our own breasts than in the enjoyment of external things;*
> *and I firmly believe it requires but a little philosophy to*
> *make a man happy in whatever state he is."*
> —Daniel Boone

What then is the relationship between pleasure and happiness? By almost all reckonings happiness is a more sustained experience of feeling good than individual pleasures. So, happiness is simply the choice to move gracefully from one experience of pleasure to another and on to another. It is the ability to feel good about most things most of the time. It is the skill of focusing on the pleasures of the moment and letting unessential concerns, particularly of the past and the future, fade into the background. Happiness is also a by-product of feeling good about ourselves. When you are feeling good about yourself, try being unhappy. I'll bet you can't do it unless you change your focus to something you don't like.

Some may regard pleasure as being selfish. The notion is that when we are only paying attention to how we feel, we are neglecting others, who are somehow more important. Doing things for others is a marvelous experience and one that deserves all the praise it gets. However, giving to others expecting a reward or fulfilling a duty is not giving at all. Being generous with time or money expecting thanks or praise is a form of barter. When we do these things because we want to, because we feel good doing them, then that feeling is reward enough. We are then being both selfish and authentic. And, it is in this selfish authenticity that we are being generous from the heart. We are creating more pleasure all around and everyone gets to feel good.

There is no question that we have achieved great things with science. By taking things apart and finding out how they work we have been able to alter DNA, fly men to the moon, and create millions of miraculous inventions and products. In using science we assume that we know why things do the things they do, what causes something else to happen. Quite naturally, we take this thinking and assume that we can figure out why things happen internally in our emotions and feelings. Then we carry that a little further and say that such-and-such events in our early life (or perhaps in earlier lives) occurred and they are what have caused the present situation. In order to have a different experience we need to somehow fix or change the impact of those prior events.

However, there is a different way to do things. We can change our lives based on our choices, choices we make in the present. And we do that by being aware of our feelings and choosing to find a better way to feel. That's where The Skills of Pleasure come in.

> "As you are feeling positive emotion—such as love, peace, happiness, joy, excitement, exhilaration…it is your Inner Being communicating to you in that moment that you are feeling the emotion—that your thoughts are in harmony with that which you are wanting, As you are experiencing negative emotion—such as fear or doubt, anger, hatred, jealousy, stress, guilt, anxiety—it is a communication from your Inner Being telling you, that in that moment, that which you are focused upon is not in harmony with what you are wanting."
>
> —Abraham-Hicks

A corollary of this is that by following our pleasures, getting to know which pleasures lead to the greatest positive feelings and which are just not satisfactory enough, we can get to know this Inner Being of ours. We can learn who we are at our deepest levels. This is one of the ways that The Skills of Pleasure develop into a very powerful spiritual path.

Many spiritual traditions begin with paying attention to our thoughts, something that can be very difficult and unpleasant if most of our thoughts involve fears. One of the most useful aspects of The Skills of Pleasure is that when we are turning our focus towards pleasure, our thoughts tend to become more pleasurable and thus much more fun to pay attention to. We then have a motivation to watch our thoughts and the act of taking responsibility for what we are thinking takes on a decidedly joyous aspect.

> *"The willingness to accept responsibility for one's own life*
> *is the source from which self-respect springs."*
> —Joan Didion

I have intentionally avoided a discussion of brain biochemistry in this book, particularly as it applies to feelings and pleasure. There are many fine books that explore this exciting subject. Our knowledge of the hormones and peptides involved in our happiness increases with great rapidity and there is much to be learned from all the tremendous science that has gone before, as well as what we have yet to discover.

However, no amount of biological understanding will enable us to choose happiness. Comprehending how we choose and seeing the effects of these choices in our own lives is the only way I know to become skilled at feeling good. This arena is very subjective; we are dealing with our own personal experience. It is for this reason that I have adopted an approach that operates from the questions, "What is my experience?" and "How can I change it?" In trying to identify the ways in which we can go from hoping that happiness comes to us, to the notion that we can take responsibility for our emotional life, I have not found a use for the concepts of neurotransmitters and the other elements of brain science here. They are quite useful in other areas, just not this one.

I need to be clear at this point about love and pleasure, and how they are related. Essentially they are the same experience. I use the word "pleasure" mostly because it has a broader range of usage than the word "love" in our language. For instance, I could just as easily say, "I love riding on a roller coaster!" as "I get enormous pleasure from riding on a roller coaster!" But to say "I love blue socks" overstates the case where I could more appropriately say, "I get great pleasure out of wearing blue socks occasionally." On the other hand, if I were to say to my beloved at the altar, "I really enjoy you!" she would likely look around for someone else who would actually "love" her. But "pleasure" encompasses feelings as diverse as simple enjoyment to ecstasy and bliss. Compassion is somewhat different from love as an experience, but both would be labeled as types of "pleasure."

I come to this work from many years of fascination with pleasure and how it works in our lives. In the 1960's I was like many young people, searching for ways to feel better in Utopian settings. It seemed so easy and wonderful then. Too bad we couldn't hold it; somehow it all dissolved away.

After college I became a chef because I got a great deal of pleasure from giving pleasure to others, especially in the form of delicious and beautiful food. One day, when I was training to be a chef, one of my teachers was giving us a lecture on the almost sacred nature of our work: to help our customers lift their moods and lighten their lives. I was so fascinated by this alchemy that I pressed him for more and more information. Finally, out of exasperation, he said to me, "What do you want, my recipe for jealousy?"

No, I didn't want the recipe for jealousy. But I did want the recipe for peace, joy, and happiness. Cooking for other people did provide moments of great magic, special times when harmony and communion reigned. But, those moments didn't last.

The great religions didn't quite do it for me either. I needed more room for self-discovery, adventure, self-empowerment, and, of course, pleasure. Tantra, at first the neo-Tantra and then the more classical varieties, appealed to me for a long time, and much of this work has Tantric roots. However, even with Tantra something seemed to be missing. It didn't quite speak to me in terms of the apparent transformation of human consciousness currently taking place.

I have been studying shamanism for about twenty-five years now and find that its focus on helping others heal—that is, to come to a place where they feel better—is very satisfying. When I found Huna, a shamanic spiritual philosophy that is of Hawaiian origin, I felt I had found the most useful, powerful, and effective system so far. It dovetailed nicely with much of the newer wisdom circulating around about creating our own reality and how we can alter our experiences of life. Shamans are people in nature-based societies who are healers working to restore harmony to relationships. These relationships can be anything from the relationship between a group and their gods, the relationship between various members of a group, or the relationship between an individual and his or her own body. Shamans work with the unseen in these healings, using whatever it takes to effect a change in the realities of the people wanting healing.

I refer to myself these days as a *Shaman of Pleasure*. I do this not so much as a marketing device, but rather to present the concept that pleasure heals. I believe that each of us can work with the unseen, at the very least our unseen subconscious and our unseen Higher Mind, to heal ourselves. We do this through restoring the harmony within to the point of feeling good. Thus, a shaman of pleasure is someone who uses pleasure for healing, whether it is for an individual or for the planet. I now teach Huna and The Skills of Pleasure regularly and have helped hundreds of people change their lives for the better through this work.

I started working on this book about seven years ago. It was fun laying out the individual skills and developing the ideas I wanted to present. But when it came time to actually write the book, I kept getting bogged down. Ironically enough, it wasn't actually a pleasure to be writing a book about pleasure. Simply put, I hadn't done all the work that needed to be done. I had to go down layer by layer into myself to get to the places where I could deeply experience each feeling I was talking about. What I have written here is my best understanding of this enormous field, simplified into seven skills that will enable you to more quickly and effectively get in touch with your feelings and to choose the ones you want.

The Skills of Pleasure are a set of talents or expertise that are constantly being honed even by even the happiest of people. They are not like a box of tools that one searches through to find just the right one for any given problem. And they are not like the different pigments on an artist's palette. They are more like the practiced abilities of a chef—using the knife safely and accurately, timing all the dishes to come out at the right moment, seasoning a dish knowing full well that the balance will change in the cooking. Or they are like the skills of tennis pro's that need to be practiced every day – the backhand, the forehand, the serve, tracking the opponent while keeping an eye on the ball. The Skills of Pleasure reward mastery enormously. Every day is different and each moment offers opportunities for new pleasures, some just opening up for the very first time.

Welcome to the Workshop of Pleasure!

Throughout this book I will be offering you short meditations or exercises that will help you put The Skills of Pleasure into practice. Here to start is a visualization where you are invited to simply look at which dishes at the Buffet of the Universe appeal to you most. You might simply read it through and notice how you feel afterwards. You might read it over again more slowly and see how you feel as you think about each item. It is simply an exercise to stimulate your feelings (and appetite) and to notice the places in your heart that yearn for more of something.

❖ THE BUFFET OF THE UNIVERSE ❖

At the Buffet of the Universe is a vast table of wondrous things to feast on. There are big mounds of light and airy joy, long cakes of deep satisfaction, shimmering bowls of jolliness, steaming tureens of sweet comfort, and great platters of delicate kindnesses. There are fat dumplings of generosity, grand salads of sacred acceptance, frothy fountains of fun, and big ornate bowls overflowing with beauty. There are assorted tartlets of curiosity, wonder, and awe, juicy berries of bliss with cream and sugar, sweet-scented pâtés of compassion and care, savory stews of success and service, and great baskets of benevolence. There are fine noodles of connection, spicy sauces of passion and excitement, rich bars of wisdom and discernment, and long, long kebobs of friendship. There are luscious pastries filled with patience and empathy, great trays of insight and understanding, enormous casks of cool forgiveness, fragrant pies of delight and pleasure, and tubs and tubs of laughter and giggles.

Enjoy your feast. You can come back for seconds and thirds. You can take some home with you. *All you need to do is choose what you want and accept it when it comes.*

SECTION I

The Nature of Pleasure

In any discussion of pleasure we need to know what pleasure really is and how it works. In this section we investigate what constitutes pleasure, the ways that we experience pleasure, how it behaves over time, the nature of desire and its connection to pleasure, and the connection of pleasure to our Higher Mind.

"People have many different kinds of pleasure. The real one is that for which they will forsake the others."
—Marcel Proust

CHAPTER 1

Looking Inside the Body of Pleasure

"Pleasure is the object, duty, and the goal of all rational creatures."
—Voltaire

Pleasure is not only our experience of enjoying something, but it is also our sense of wellbeing, our sense of being healthy and alive, and our sense of loving and being loved. Each day we go through the habits that we have designed to maximize our pleasure while we get things done. Our morning routines are created to get us up and on our way with the least amount of stress and with as much pleasure as we can muster. Perhaps we add to that pleasure by looking forward to some accomplishment, and perhaps even the pleasure of connecting with friends. We anticipate the pleasure of coming home again and relaxing in our favorite ways. In the course of a day we may exercise because we like the way it makes us feel. We may read a newspaper or watch the news because we like feeling connected to the world and we like the sense of knowing what's going on. We have relationships with people because we enjoy connecting to them. Some will make us laugh; some will make us cry. But, if we truly connect with them, they all make us feel good.

However, it's easy to misunderstand pleasure. It is often viewed as something that is both desirable and good in moderation, but also as something that is dangerous, potentially leading to addictions, emotional difficulties, ethical problems, or spiritual suffering. Plato said it plainly, "Pleasure is the greatest incentive to evil." It comes and it goes, and when it goes, so say some, it leaves us aching for more, which is very unpleasant. That same common wisdom says that pain always follows pleasure; that pleasure is invariably wrapped up in suffering and thus the wise would avoid it altogether. How very sad!

Those people who seek lots of pleasure are often dismissed as "hedonists," suggesting the obsessive pursuit of pleasure at the expense of other "more important" things. The pursuit of pleasure is regarded as a mindless folly and the means whereby fortunes and health are lost. Wisdom, from this viewpoint, is knowing just how much pleasure we can allow ourselves to have without falling into its many traps.

What all of these critics miss is that *everything* we do is about pleasure. We may not get the pleasure we're after, but our motivation is always towards more pleasure and less pain. The "trick," if you will, is to understand *all* of our pleasures and to not overlook some of our significant pleasures that are obscured by more immediate ones.

Treating pleasure like a tempting siren luring us to our doom is like saying that marriage is a certain pathway to misery and tears. It's not the experience itself that is the problem; it's how we handle it. We can take it as it comes and hope for the best. Or we can learn how it works, see what makes it work well, and learn to develop it skillfully.

The question is, how can we do this? That, of course, is what this book is about and we start by observing how pleasure works.

> *"Listen closely. I want to tell you the best-kept health secret on the planet. Ready? Here it is: Pleasure is an essential nutrient that you need, each and every day, to become and remain healthy."*
> —Christiane Northrup, M.D.

First, there are several common patterns that we can notice. These patterns help us predict what activities will be pleasurable and may help explain why some experiences aren't as pleasurable as we think they should be.

These patterns—tension and release, contrast and novelty, and the pleasure trajectory—also help us understand why pleasures come to an end. We can more easily let go of a given pleasure as it winds down when we have accepted *at the outset* that it won't go on forever.

TENSION AND RELEASE

Stephen is outside having fun playing catch with his friends. Rachel is sitting on the sidelines watching the boys, eating an ice cream cone, and talking with her girl friends. Howard looks out his window at the kids as he takes a moment's break from his project of redesigning his kitchen, and smiles. Monica is cheerfully ignoring them all in her quiet space as she meditates. All four members of this family are enjoying themselves; they are experiencing pleasure. Yet each is doing something very different. What is it that is common to their experiences so that we can say each is feeling pleasure?

One key element to pleasure is that it is about tension and release—the greater the tension, the greater the release, and thus the greater the pleasure. Stephen repeatedly tenses to catch the ball and releases that tension when he does so. He then tenses as he throws the ball and relaxes while the other boy tries to catch it. Rachel tenses slightly as she desires and anticipates the next bite of ice cream. She relaxes when she senses that creamy sweetness in her mouth. She tenses with excitement as she and her friends talk about their other friends and releases that tension in giggles and laughter. Howard tenses when he encounters a problem in his design and relaxes when he solves it. He tenses when he thinks about the children's safety and relaxes when he sees that they are okay. Monica is simply becoming aware of tensions that have accumulated over the years and is relaxing them one by one. Each member of the family is enjoying this natural process.

Scary things like horror movies and roller coasters build high tension intentionally so that there will be a great release at some point.

That's a large part of why they're fun. Without that release of tension they would be very unpleasant. Tension without release is painful. Danger, for instance, can add pleasure to an erotic situation by increasing the tension. But that only works when there is a point when that danger disappears and everyone can relax.

Contrast and Variety

> *"Variety is the soul of pleasure."*
> —Aphra Behn

> *"Pleasure is none, if not diversified."*
> —John Donne

Pleasure can also be seen as largely a function of contrasts. A lot of one kind of food either at one time or in succession quickly loses its pleasurable qualities, whereas a buffet with lots of different offerings can be delightful. Music works best with contrasts of melody and harmony, softness and loudness, and varying rhythms. Paintings also rely on contrast, that of colors and textures. Sensual touch only feels good if the giver moves around and gives a variety of sensations. Games are only fun if sometimes we win and sometimes we lose. Too much of one or the other becomes boring and unpleasant.

So a main component of pleasure is about change. It is never static. It is constantly evolving. The first sip of a cold drink on a sweltering day is generally the very best one because it is in the greatest contrast to the hot, dry experience just before it. Similarly, we love vacations because they are different from our usual lives.

Now obviously, some of the things we have or do are very familiar to us and the pleasure of these things is not immediately obvious as change. We may desire comfort food, for example, or the feeling of an old favorite chair. But when we want these things, generally it's because we have had enough of things that are stressful and we want something calming and nurturing. The stark contrast is what makes it particularly pleasurable.

THE PLEASURE TRAJECTORY

Pleasure isn't a thing that one grabs onto, enjoys for a while, and then drops along the way. Pleasure is an experience of perception that has a natural, predictable pattern. It starts at a low level, rises to some kind of height or peak, and then trails off to nothing. This trajectory can take place in a matter of moments or over the course of years. There may be periods when there are little peaks and valleys, only to return to an increase in intensity. Likewise there may be similar little peaks as the overall intensity subsides. But the basic pattern remains: pleasure rises, peaks, and subsides.

So the experience of any given pleasure is going to come to an end. Period. There is no getting around it any more than we can stay in childhood forever or keep jumping up without coming down. If we can recognize that that is the nature of pleasure, then we don't have to get upset when the pleasure comes to an end. We knew at the very beginning that it would.

Yes, we like something, and, yes, we want to have more of those yummy feelings. The way, then, to continue feeling that good is not to hang on to the fading glory of a precious moment. It is to continually find other things to feel good about. When one pleasure comes to an end, we look for another. There are potential pleasures all around us, all the time, so we start and complete the pleasure trajectory over and over.

PLEASURE AS CURRENCY

One of the many interesting things about pleasure is that we use it as an important tool every day of our lives. It is how we compare the desirability of two or more potential experiences. By using our imagination, we "feel into" how much pleasure we can expect to experience with each potential choice. It is like a currency in that it allows us to compare the value of different things easily. Three apples at 40 cents each has the same "value" as four oranges at 30 cents each. In everyday terms of decision-making, the option with the most overall pleasure wins.

When we go to a restaurant, we choose from the menu based on what choices we imagine will give us the most pleasure at that moment. Even the influence of the cost of various dishes is usually factored in to the pleasure. That is, will the cost of such-and-such a dish detract from the overall pleasure I expect to receive? Or is my sense of the value of said dish worth the cost? When we are relaxed we effortlessly evaluate several potentials at once and can quickly say what our preference is.

If, for example, I need to choose whether to go to the beach, repaint my bathroom, or visit my ailing Aunt Agatha, I will do so based on the overall pleasure I expect to receive from each choice. Going to the beach may be just what I need to relax from a stressful week at work. It would take my mind off the unsolved problems I have and it might be really fun. On the other hand the bathroom paint is falling off in places and it depresses me to go in there. I want to feel good about my bathroom again. And, on the other, other hand I have a great affection for my Aunt Agatha, and it would feel good to see the joy in her eyes when I walked into her house. All of these choices can be compared to one another because we can look into each one and get a sense of both current and potential pleasures. The relative degree of pleasure I can anticipate, the currency, is the only means I have for making a choice that will feel the best to me.

Pleasure and Numbness

It is generally easy to distinguish between pleasure and pain. We like the feelings of pleasure and we don't like the feelings of pain. However, if we can reduce the feelings of pain, is that automatically pleasure? To the degree that it actively feels good, yes. To the degree that what we are experiencing is numbness, then probably not. And it's not always easy to know the difference.

> *"I learned to be with myself rather than avoiding myself with limiting habits; I started to be aware of my feelings more, rather than numb them."*
>
> —Judith Wright

Let's say I come home tired from a long and stressful day at work. I desperately want to relax and release all the tension I've built up during the day. After popping a cold beer, I sit down in front of the television to unwind. Of course, there's a lot of pleasure in doing something different, something which does not require me to tense up to solve any problems, or deal with other people's issues, or examine my own successes and failures. But after awhile I am no longer involved in doing something different. I am allowing myself to be distracted from my own life almost entirely. I may laugh at a sitcom or cry during a soap opera. I may get a little excited watching a movie of sexy people on the screen. But while I may very well enjoy being entertained, very little of me is really engaged.

The intensity of pleasure is relatively low and, in fact, being distracted away from our tensions does not substantially release those tensions. Those tensions are merely hidden for a while. Though that may feel better than the pain of unreleased tension, it is not the same as pleasure. Another example would be drinking alcohol in large quantities. The pleasures of drinking fade as the numbing effect of the alcohol enters the brain. At the point that we're feeling no pain, we're also feeling no pleasure.

One way of distinguishing pleasure from numbness is that numbness does not follow the same patterns as pleasure. Numbness feels static, there's no sense of change in intensity or focus. Numbness doesn't build in excitement, nor is there any sense of release—just less awareness of pain. Sometimes that's just what we want. There are times when we all need relief from tensions that we can't figure out how to deal with and release. A good example might be the pain one feels when a romantic relationship just comes to an end. Some kind of painkiller may seem to be called for, but it is not the same as pleasure.

Another way to look at it is to see how the pleasure is being used. More accurately, we look at what the intention is of the activity that usually is pleasurable. For example, drinking wine with a meal can be a very pleasurable experience. However, when one drinks a lot of wine for the feeling of a buzz, then there is no focus on pleasure itself, but rather the experience of numbness. When the focus on gambling becomes about the high of the excitement and the potential for a great high in winning as a way of not being aware of other less glorious feelings, then the activity is about numbing and not one about pleasure. If we can't savor it, how can we call it a pleasure?

Numbing keeps us from our feelings. It prevents us from being aware of all that's going on in our inner world. It may be better, perhaps a lot better, than feeling negatively about ourselves and what we are doing with our lives. But there are better ways of working through those dark feelings to get back to truly enjoying life.

PLEASURE AND THE IMAGINATION

"Imagination is everything. It is the preview of life's coming attractions."
—Albert Einstein

Imagination plays a very big role in the world of pleasure. For many, their pleasures are primarily experienced in the imagination. All of advertising is about imagined pleasures. With the skilled help of the ad creators, in our imagination we get to feel what the actors or models seem to be feeling. The adventure, romance, and drama on television are all genuinely experienced vicariously through our imagination and identification with one or more of the characters. The circumstances are fictitious; as we watch we are not actually experiencing those wildly dangerous (or wildly romantic) events. However, there is a physiological response in us as though we were. Just because we can turn off the television and say to ourselves, "Oh, that wasn't real. It was just a made-up story acted out for my entertainment," doesn't mean that we didn't feel excitement or sadness or longing. We did feel something; we wouldn't have watched it if we didn't, unless we were simply numbing out. And those feelings, those inner sensations are real.

"Of course it is happening inside your head, Harry, but why on earth should that mean that it is not real?"
(Dumbledore to Harry in Harry Potter and the Deathly Hallows*)*
—J. K. Rowling

We use imagination whenever we think about what we are going to do next. We visualize nearly every action to some degree before we do it. We choose this or that action and with that momentary imagination we see a little way into the results of that choice. Perhaps it's only for a split second, but sometimes it's enough to change our minds in time before we do something really unfortunate.

As we all know, very often we get more pleasure during the anticipation of some event than we do with the actual event itself. How many times have you gotten very excited about a date, only to be somewhat disappointed with the date itself? Or expect to really enjoy a new gadget, article of clothing, or toy, only to be disappointed that it didn't quite make you feel as good as you thought it would?

As we have seen, pleasure is a constantly changing experience that has some observable attributes that help us get to know it better. In fact, not only is pleasure always changing, its very nature is about change. It is the enjoyment of things in our world shifting and growing, and the contrast with other pieces of our world. Pleasure is an important and constantly used tool for us in helping us make choices. It is quite different from the experience of numbness. And it is experienced as much in our imagination as through our physical senses.

❖ WARMING UP YOUR IMAGINATION ❖

This is a little exercise to stimulate your imagination. Just consider these ideas for a bit and see where they take you. Most of the time we start sentences with "What if…" when we are afraid. But right now take a few moments looking at one or more of these "What if…"s that are about pleasure.

- What if I could make a living doing the creative things I love to do?
- What if I had all the money I needed to travel to the places I want to see?
- What if I could live in a house that seemed just perfect?
- What if I lived a life of peace and harmony?

- What if I had a lover that knew what I liked so well that I could surrender to him or her and simply let myself be loved?

Before we start getting skilled at bringing more pleasure into our lives, we need to consider a few principles first. These principles are like rich chicken or vegetable stock that we can make a great soup or sauce from. They are like the tennis strokes we build a game around. They are like the good soil we plant our prized flowers in. Once they are in place we can focus on the more interesting or complex aspects, but they need to be there to begin with. That is the subject of the next chapter.

CHAPTER 2

Laying a Foundation for Pleasure

"Build this day on a foundation of pleasant thoughts. Never fret at any imperfection that you fear may impede your progress. Remind yourself, as often as necessary, that you are a creature of God and have the power to achieve any dream by lifting up your thoughts. You can fly when you decide that you can. Never consider yourself defeated again. Let the vision in your heart be in your life's blueprint. Smile!"

—Zig Ziglar

Some years ago I bought an abandoned restaurant from the bank in the small town on the coast of Maine where I had summered for many years. I was looking for a place to manufacture the gourmet specialty foods I was developing. I remember looking it over as thoroughly as I knew how and deciding that since all the angles looked right and there didn't seem to be any obvious rot, it was probably an okay deal. But it was up on concrete blocks, rather than having a solid cement foundation. Over the years I owned it, I ended up putting a lot more money into its upkeep than I could afford and learned a big lesson in foundations – have a solid one before you build.

In this case, we want to have a solid foundation of understanding before we start our exploration of the ways to build a life of greater joy and happiness. So we begin with the principles that underpin this approach to pleasure.

Principles are assumptions we make about life. In this case, we have observations about pleasure that give us some perspective about how we are experiencing it. These principles provide a valuable context in which we can see the shapes and contrasts of pleasure more clearly. It's like the difference between looking at a fishing hook by itself and seeing one on the end of a line with a fish on it. The hook hasn't changed, but now we see how it fits into our world.

THE FIRST PRINCIPLE OF PLEASURE: PLEASURE IS ONLY EXPERIENCED IN THE PRESENT MOMENT.

"One of the most tragic things I know about human nature is that all of us tend to put off living. We are all dreaming of some magical rose garden over the horizon—instead of enjoying the roses that are blooming outside our windows today."

—Dale Carnegie

This principle is really about how we inhabit the wonderland of feelings. These strange, often powerful, sometimes fleeting—sometimes annoyingly persistent, little morsels of life are the elements of experience. Life without feelings would be like the proverbial stone soup: there's not really anything there until we add something we can taste.

We are aware of our feelings in our bodies; that's the territory of feelings. And the body is very much tied up with what's happening right now. Our minds may be off in other realms, but our bodies stay put, both physically and temporally. So to enjoy something, which means having a pleasant physical reaction, we must be aware of our bodies experiencing something in the immediate present.

This is important to us because it makes it clear that all the mental dramas and concerns we tend to play with can effectively distract us from nurturing our pleasure. Knowing where in time to place our focus allows us to be mindful of what's genuinely important to us.

And what about past pleasures? All memories of pleasures in the past are experienced right now. Memory is a current event even though the memory is about something that has already been experienced. Just as the memory of something distinctly unpleasant recreates the unpleasant feelings, often in an endless loop, the memory of something very pleasant is a distinct experience, different from the experience that is remembered. For instance, the memory of a wonderful summer picnic with a new love, as delicious as it is, is not the same event as the picnic itself. It is something related, but different. By recognizing the difference we can become aware of this new event, the recreation of the picnic in the present, and remain aware of ourselves in our current circumstances at the same time.

Being present also relieves us of the burdens of the past. When we have regrets we are remembering things that have happened before and our feelings about those memories can make us feel sad, ashamed, guilty, or lonely. While these feelings arise according to how we tell our stories of the past, they are incapable of arising at all when we are fully focused on what's happening in the present moment.

In the same way, we cannot experience fear when we are fully present. All fear is about the future. Without that focus on the future we are without fear. I'm not suggesting that we shouldn't consider the future and look at what options we have to influence the experiences to come. What I am suggesting is that we avoid getting caught up in fear by staying in the present as much as possible. Many great spiritual teachers have emphasized the virtue of staying in the present moment, in large measure as a way of preventing the debilitating effects of fear. And becoming aware of the things around us that we enjoy is one of the easiest and most effective ways of immediately coming back into the present moment.

> *"We know nothing of tomorrow; our business is*
> *to be good and happy today."*
> —Sydney Smith

Allowing our focus to rest in the present, to remain aware of only what is in front of us, not only avoids difficult feelings, it is also a very pleasant feeling on its own. It is truly one of the great pleasures of life. Being present to the whole experience of our first cup of tea or coffee in the morning is much more enjoyable than just the tea or coffee itself. Being present to the morning is a delight all its own. Being present to our love of a child or a pet is another great joy. These are examples of savoring, of course. But they are also examples of presence. And often-times we can be present to ourselves without any particular focus. It is for that particular pleasure that many people enjoy meditating. By just being aware of ourselves in this moment, gently maintaining a focus on the experience of living, can be an extraordinary feeling. Genuine presence simply feels good.

> *"Do not dwell in the past, do not dream of the future,*
> *concentrate the mind on the present moment."*
> —Buddha

And sometimes even being present to pain is a pleasure of sorts. By relaxing the fear that usually accompanies pain, we can just be aware of the intensity. For those people who have shut down their feelings for one reason or another, this can be a good step towards returning to fully feeling. I have witnessed a number of people who have used pain, or a least intense sensation, as a way of finding their way back to an acceptance of feeling. There is a pleasure in being so deeply present to the experience that they can have both feelings at once, the feeling of pain/intensity and the feeling of the pleasure of presence.

> *"The highest ecstasy is the attention at its fullest."*
> —Simone Weil

So by being aware that it is only in the present moment that we can experience pleasure, and, as a corollary, that feeling pleasure brings us back into the moment, we can access the power of pleasure. When we are enjoying our lives, feeling good about life and who we are, we are in our most potent place.

The Second Principle of Pleasure: We Can Choose How We Feel.

"While we may not be able to control all that happens to us,
we can control what happens inside us."
—Benjamin Franklin

For many of us the world of feelings is relatively foreign. They are often regarded as awkward experiences that get in the way of living our lives. This is especially apparent when someone does something that we don't like and we find ourselves reacting to that person in very negative ways.

But the mechanisms of feelings are fairly straightforward. For the most part, feelings are predicated on thoughts. We usually have to fully feel what's going on, but having done that, we can intentionally change our thoughts and thus we can change how we feel.

That sounds simple enough, but what gets tricky is being aware of what we are thinking at any given moment. Paying attention to our thoughts is a whole new ballgame for some. For others, those thoughts are such a jumbled circus that there seems no way to spot one thought in the midst of so many others.

Even trickier are the thoughts that have become so ingrained that we now call them beliefs. These beliefs become a part of our reality and thus seem to be indistinguishable from "the true nature of things." We build our reality on how we interpret our experience. If we get burned at the stove as a child, we learn that fire hurts, that stoves have fire, and that it's smart and less painful to stay away from stoves. Later we learn that we can work with a stove safely and that it's a useful thing to do. We have changed our rules of reality regarding fire and stoves.

We have so many rules of reality that we don't realize that they're there. Since everyone around us has more or less the same rules of reality, our part in the creation of reality doesn't get noticed. But each of us has an operating system that lets us build upon basic assumptions to create a workable life. If that workable life isn't as great as we might like it to be becomes irrelevant. At least it seems that way. Shit happens and life is the way it is, etc.

Taking things a step further, when our view of reality is threatened, we often become disturbed and seek to blame some one or some thing else for threatening our world. We can become outraged when some part of the world is not meeting our expectations. When the world around us changes dramatically, we can become severely shocked. When someone dies, for instance, we can experience great grief because of the violence done to our inner world.

What we forget is that all those rules of reality were either created by us or adopted by us. Naturally our parents, our schools, our friends, and the media all had a part in telling us what is and what isn't. But we had the choice to accept it or fight it. Fighting it may not have made much sense when we were young, since we didn't have enough information to make a different choice, nor did we have the power to meaningfully rebel. So we may have accepted a great many things that we, as adults, can now see aren't really the way we were taught.

"As far as the laws of mathematics refer to reality, they are not certain, and as far as they are certain, they do not refer to reality."
—Albert Einstein

For instance, many people in my generation were taught that race was an important distinction in how you treated other people. The same was true with gender. That notion is not as influential now as it was then, but it still is a rule of reality that many people hold. Another rule of reality that we were taught is that science "knows" just about everything and that there are very clear rules of physics that form the foundation of all science. Now, the quantum physicists are in disagreement with the implications of their discoveries of such phenomena as non-locality (two related things happening far apart in places where there is no physical connection), antimatter, and probability waves. And, most disturbing of all, is the apparent influence of consciousness on what becomes reality and what doesn't.

*"We are not animals. We are not a product of what has happened
to us in our past. We have the power of choice."*

—Stephen Covey

When we have an experience, we are given the choice of how we will react to it, and that in turn will determine how we feel. For instance, if my partner of many years decides that it's time for this relationship to be over, I am presented with lots of options. I can choose to think that my world is falling apart, and thus feel crushed—unhappy, lonely, grieving, disconsolate, etc. Or, I can choose to be grateful for the time we had together, and see it as an opportunity to create an even better life for myself. There are many other possible choices, but the point is that I have a choice over how I think about this new situation.

That we have patterns of thinking that we have used most of our lives doesn't mean that that's the way things have to be. By choosing ways of thinking that make us feel good, we increase the level of happiness in our lives.

Some may say that I'm fooling around with reality and that I either I'm not being realistic or I'm just playing Pollyanna (the young girl who always saw things from the bright side in the story by Eleanor H. Porter). If we make the assumption that life is tough, dangerous, and hard, then perhaps they're right. But we don't have to make that assumption. We could just as easily make the assumption, a belief, that life is beautiful, loving, and fun. One assumption is not more correct than the other. It's entirely up to us what assumptions we make. Whatever assumption we do make will determine how we view life and thus how we experience life.

Happiness is a choice. Once we decide to be happy, the decisions we make along the way will be more in alignment with our happiness. Without the decision to be happy we're like Dorothy in *The Wizard of Oz*. She had the power to go home all along, but it took a great many adventures to come to a place where she could believe that.

"A man is happy so long as he chooses to be happy
and nothing can stop him."
—Alexander Solzenitsyn

THE THIRD PRINCIPLE OF PLEASURE: PLEASURE SHOWS US WHEN WE ARE BECOMING ALIGNED WITH OUR CORE BEING.

These Principles of Pleasure are really about the context of pleasure in our lives. When we zoom out and look at our experiences of pleasure, what are we seeing going on around these experiences? It isn't just a mass of wonderful feelings that are caused by some random events. Our whole being participates in the experience. And that whole being includes our bodies, our conscious mind, and that greater part of us that we call spirit or soul. A sense of wellbeing pervades all of us.

That a sense of connection to this transcendent part of us feels good is fairly obvious. As I mentioned earlier, all religions are about pleasure: the deeper the connection, actually to anything, the greater the pleasure. What may not be so obvious is that pleasure is a sign of our connection. That is to say, when we are genuinely feeling pleasure we are experiencing a connection with our spirit or soul.

It is this experience that shows us the connection between pleasure and our deeper parts. These deeper parts are where we find our power, our wisdom, our meaning, even our health. So, by being aware of our level of pleasure, we are also noting our level of connectedness to these deeper parts.

"Physical pleasure is a sensual experience no different from pure seeing
or the pure sensation with which a fine fruit fills the tongue; it is a great
unending experience, which is given us, a knowing of the world, the
fullness and the glory of all knowing."
—Rainer Maria Rilke

It's fairly easy to notice that when we are feeling pretty rotten, either physically or emotionally, we are also feeling pretty disconnected from our deeper parts. The world seems to close in and our inner focus gets very narrow. Nothing much matters except that we find a way to start feeling better.

When we go from a place of feeling terrible to one of just feeling bad it is progress. It is feeling better. Feeling better, particularly better about oneself, is getting closer to the sense of being connected to spirit. Thus, every pleasure, even if it is a pleasure at the lower end of the scale, is a step towards our own divinity. The pleasure itself is a signal that we are moving in the right direction.

Feeling good about ourselves is the experience of being connected to our deeper parts. This is such a valuable understanding that I recommend going inside and investigating this for yourself. For when we can make the connection for ourselves between pleasure and our core being (or whatever we have chosen to call it), then we have the basis for our own inner guidance system.

The inner guidance system works simply by paying attention to how we feel, realizing that that is an answer from our core being. For instance, if I were to ask, in any fashion, whether if what I am contemplating is in alignment with my core being, I might get a "yes" reverberating in my mind, I might see some positive symbol, or I might get some sound like trumpets or a choir of angels. But most likely I will simply get a feeling sense that feels good. A mild excitement or a feeling of being more energized might be how I experience it. Very simply, feeling good is a sign of being in alignment and feeling bad is a sign of being out of alignment.

We need to be careful here; wording the question right is important. If I ask if it is in my best long-term interest to date this person who excites me, I may well get a positive response. However, if I put in a time factor, like dating her before she gets a divorce, then I might get a negative response.

Another example might be asking if now is the appropriate time to leave my job for another one. Perhaps it is in the sense that it would be valuable to start looking around to see what's out there, but not to quit today. Either a positive or negative response wouldn't really tell me much. It might be better to put it in general terms and ask if I would be wise to start the process now of moving on.

These answers are coming from an intelligence that doesn't use language as its primary way of communicating. We are asking questions with our mind, but we are also putting information out there about what we are interested in with our feelings. Putting our question in terms of a picture, a visualization, as in picturing the scenario we are contemplating, and then being aware of what feelings arise with that picture should give us a good answer. We do need to give it some time, though. There may be multiple feelings coming forth.

This is not a predictive method as such. What is going to happen isn't something that is out there that a higher being, albeit your own, can see but you can't. This is about you choosing what happens, but asking first what information your core has for you about your choice.

These principles support our understanding of pleasure like the three legs of a stool. They answer three basic questions: Where do we find pleasure? What do we need in order to find it? What does it look like when we do find it?

Simply put, we find pleasure in the present moment. We need to accept responsibility for how we feel. And it looks like the very essence of who we are.

❖ REMEMBERING OUR DEEPEST CONNECTIONS ❖

Think of the last time you felt deeply connected to something. It may have been out in nature. Perhaps it was in a religious or intentionally spiritual setting. Or maybe it was with someone very vulnerable, like a very young child or someone close to dying. Let yourself explore the feelings of that memory. There were probably many different things going on inside you. Can you identify any of them?

How do you like those feelings?

These principles form the underpinnings of this approach to pleasure. They provide us with insight into what we can do with pleasure and how it is more than simply feeling good. The Skills of Pleasure, which in turn lead us to the Power of Pleasure, carry on from these simple principles. But before we go there, a little trip through Desire is in order.

CHAPTER 3

The Nature and Function of Desire

"Desire is the very essence of man."
—Baruch Spinoza

We can't really speak about pleasure without bringing in desire; they are the great dancing duo of the emotional world. Desire steps forward first, often with a pronounced flourish, demanding that pleasure come out to dance with him. When pleasure does appear, desire steps back and allows pleasure to shine for as long as she can. And when pleasure has shown what she has, she fades back into the shadows and desire comes forth again with a new summons to the dance floor.

This is the balance between enjoyment and desire; they act in tandem. We can enjoy something now, but at some point that pleasure diminishes. And when it does, that sense of not-good-enough sets in. That's when desire leads us on to the next pleasure, to change what is happening in some way, to once again enjoy things. The natural rhythm is desire, creation of some way to satisfy the desire, enjoyment of the fruits of that creation, the fading of the pleasure, and the arising of a new desire.

In this chapter we will look at some of the elements of this dance: gratification, urges, lust, attractions, dissatisfaction, and Calls to Wholeness. As we sit in our front row seats, we will have an opportunity to witness one of nature's most majestic performances—the passionate dance of desires and pleasures.

THE ROLE OF DESIRE

Desire is how the system works; everything we do is based on a desire, a desire to somehow feel better than how we are feeling right now. We go from moment to moment, always evaluating competing desires on the basis of what will bring us the most overall pleasure. Some of those desires allow for a postponement of the fulfillment of those desires. Some even accept that there will be a certain amount of pain involved as well, if the potential pleasure is great enough. But we can't escape from desire, for even wanting to have no desires is a desire itself.

And there is nothing wrong with desires. The world would never change if there were no desires. Perhaps the world would even stop turning if there were no desires, because desires begin the acts of all that is alive. Plants desire more sun and grow in that direction. Plants and animals desire food and will do whatever they possibly can to get it. It might be stretching things a bit, but it seems that the wind is filled with desire, always moving on, trying to get to somewhere else. With the help of gravity, water always "seeks" its own level. Fire has a ravenous appetite, a passionate desire to consume things. And stones and rocks seem to desire only to be left alone to their peace and quiet.

"Desire is the starting point of all achievement, not a hope, not a wish, but a keen pulsating desire which transcends everything."
—Napoleon Hill

Every desire is important, no matter how base or trivial. Each little desire is a step towards fulfilling our grandest and deepest desires. The whole point of desires is to explore, to have experiences, and to discover more about who we are. Even if all we desire is to do what we have done a thousand times, if we feel the desire, we have not finished with it.

When we desire something, it is not always obvious what makes it so desirable. I suspect that it is the rare person who reflects on why he wants a new car or why she craves a new dress. These desires, any desires really, may require substantial effort to be fulfilled. So what is the real payoff for all that work? It is feeling good, especially feeling good about oneself.

Like most things in life, there are multiple levels to desire. At one level, a desire is to do, be, or have something. At another level, less obvious, the desire is about attaining a very good feeling. At yet another level, desires are about exploring the essence of our being. They are about the adventure of life. They are the ways in which we grow as humans. We become something more with each desire that gets acted upon. That, of course, doesn't mean that we are always happy with the results of our fulfilled desires. But like a scientific experiment, we learn more about how to get what we want, if only how not to go about it. That is the basis of wisdom.

GRATIFICATION

The experience of gratification is one of satisfaction, like scratching an itch or releasing a long held weight. It is the pleasure of relieving the tension built up by a desire. There is a sense of wellbeing associated with gratification, it is the feeling that at least this one thing has happened and that it can now be enjoyed. There is something in gratification that nourishes the soul, often expressed as "Ahhhhh!"

Unfortunately, gratification has been made to seem unworthy by expressions like, "instant gratification." This is the notion that the immediate gratification of some desire takes away the will to postpone present pleasure in favor of a later fulfillment of another, presumably more important, desire. This makes a "virtue" of deferred gratification and patience. While a sense of proportion and perspective is very useful in developing a strategy for maximizing personal pleasure, gratification itself is something to be savored.

> *"The gratification comes in the doing, not in the results."*
> —James Dean

The word "gratify" comes with the olden meaning of "to reward" or "remunerate." In our context here, it is the pleasure reward for the fulfillment of a desire. But it is also the awareness of pleasure in the moment, as in the James Dean quote. Gratification, in the sense of that soul nourishment, is available all the time. It is a perspective on the value of any instant, whether that instant is one of the culmination of something or just the joy of being present in the moment.

DESIRES AND ATTRACTIONS

They are obviously related, but there is a subtle difference between desires and attractions. Desire wants to be, do, or have something. Attraction is the feeling that we are powerfully drawn to some thing or some person. It is often for unknown reasons, as in some sexual attractions, but the experience is that of unseen forces at work pulling at us to make certain kinds of connections that satisfy some deep part of us. We most often think of attractions in terms of love and sex, but we can just as easily be attracted to powerful people, meaningful artwork, magnetic ideas, or perhaps those we feel are in need of our special help.

It's easy to overlook the rich material we are presented with each day in the form of our attractions. Why are we attracted to certain people, or certain types of people? Why do we crave certain things? Why do specific objects, ideas, or dreams have a kind of mystical power over us? I would suggest that these are all Calls to Wholeness. They are experiences that we are drawn to that will help us explore who we are and that at a Soul level they help us come into greater alignment with our deepest core.

It doesn't mean that by eating that gallon of Rocky Road ice cream we've been craving, we will become enlightened. However, it does suggest that if we are drawn to eating a gallon of Rocky Road, there is something there that we are being called to learn or explore. In this example, we may be invited to learn that it's okay to totally indulge ourselves once in a while. It may be that the lesson has to do with learning the effects of over-indulging ourselves. Or it may be that the primary lesson is learning how to best evaluate all of our desires together in order to maximize our pleasure. This would involve understanding the consequences of fulfilling one of our desires completely to the exclusion of others, and also to learn how to find the right mix of pleasure now versus pain later. So the eating of a gallon of Rocky Road may well not be about right and wrong but about discernment, how well we understand how to use our natural guidance system, which is, in itself, about feeling our way towards wholeness.

CALLS TO WHOLENESS

> *"Individuality is only possible if it unfolds from wholeness."*
> —David Bohm

When we believe that we are not enough—not beautiful enough, wealthy enough, or perfect enough—a great many of our desires revolve around becoming truly "enough." This is the basic desire of our Soul, to hear the Calls to Wholeness and come back into the fullness of our being.

There was a magnificent garden in my dreams recently. It was the most vibrantly colorful garden imaginable. The reds and yellows were shockingly deep and powerful. The background colors of blue and green were like the deep songs of whales made visual. It was intensity itself, clothed in color and shape. I reacted to it by being grateful that I had found it again and couldn't understand how I could have lost it. It was a clear recognition that I both knew it well and profoundly yearned to return to it.

Finding paradise, losing it again, and struggling to come back to it once more is the stuff of great novels. Once we get a taste of it, nothing else will do. It calls to us like the Bali Hai of *South Pacific*, saying, "Come to me, come to me."

Science has us focus on cause and effect as though the present has predictably appeared, inexorably driven from the past. This idea looks at life mechanically, where each moment is the sum of all the moments before it. But this ignores the very powerful ways that we are called to do or be something. From somewhere beyond any discernable past, new ideas and desires pull at us like an insistent little child. This tug is irresistible. We can delay it or fight against it, but we can't hold it off forever. It's as though our future was summoning us to become who we were meant to be. Science doesn't have room for this, but our hearts do.

So these calls from the future, or wherever, challenge us; they challenge us to become something different. They never seem to invite us into a place of comfort or indolence. It's always some place that is at least a little uncomfortable, a little disorienting, and potentially much more pleasurable.

The great motivator of life—desire—whispers to us in dreams, like mine. It appears as chance words from a friend or a book. Or it reveals itself in works of art or nature. Sometimes soft words or images suddenly appear in our psyche. These subtle messages promise us something more though, than just the experience of soon-to-be-attained pleasure. There is something in each message that says, "Follow me back to yourself." It's as though we're called by those pieces of ourselves that have been lost or neglected to bring them home.

"You are all things. Denying, rejecting, judging or hiding from any aspect of your total being creates pain and results in a lack of wholeness."
—Joy Page

Wholeness feels good. Each time we welcome some long-lost piece of ourselves home and accept it into our heart, we experience a rush of pleasure. It could be a sigh of relief at the letting go of some long held resistance. It could be the surprise of seeing some unknown aspect of our personality. It could be an orgasm of epic proportions that has been waiting to come out for years.

But some attractions defy easy understanding, like pedophilia, kleptomania, and self-destructive behaviors. We can make the assumption that those people who experience these kinds of attractions are somehow defective and we need to either "fix" them or marginalize them. Or we can make the assumption that what these people are experiencing is a call to their own personal wholeness, however strange it looks to us. As a society we must have enforceable laws that protect innocent people from the *actions* of other people, whatever it is that those people may be trying to heal. But, when we start judging other people's *feelings*, we are no longer safe to feel what's going on within us. By assuming that all feelings are there for a reason, we are free to explore who we are, safely. We are free to answer our own Calls to Wholeness.

OUR SEXUAL FANTASIES

Some of our greatest Calls to Wholeness are our sexual fantasies. When we allow ourselves to fully feel our sexual fantasies, if and when we have them, they provide us with amazing feelings and insight into our greater being. One insight is that the feeling of immense turn-on is the same feeling as the feeling we have when we feel really, really good about ourselves. As *Star Trek*'s Mr. Spock might say, "Fascinating!"

That being who fills us with such longing, that radiantly sexy person, real or imagined, who excites us so, is a glorious reflection of the spectacular nature of our own core self. Whether or not we actually pursue that person, it's useful to see both them and ourselves in this light. They teach us how wonderful *we* really are.

Some fantasies are amenable to acting out in some fashion. With a willing partner and the right kind of place, acting out some sexual fantasies can be immensely satisfying fun. But some sexual fantasies seem darker and not appropriate for real world play. That doesn't mean there's anything wrong with them as fantasies. We just need to see them for what they are: Calls to Wholeness.

Exploring our sexual fantasies is like dancing with a part of us that is normally left sitting off to the side. The characters in these fantasies are like those in any dream; they are us, aspects of ourselves that may not be as socially acceptable as other aspects. Very possibly, we have a negative attitude towards these inner characters. Shame, guilt, feelings of unworthiness, and jealousy all stop pleasure dead in its tracks. But they don't affect desire. Sexual fantasies and the characters in them that are affected by these pleasure-killers just get compartmentalized. They live on, in a different room within. They are fun to play with but we can't take them out in public.

> *"Fantasy mirrors desire. Imagination shapes it."*
> —Mason Cooley

It's like *Beauty and the Beast*. There is some part of us that seems to have been cursed. Of course, in this case we have cursed that part ourselves. If that part of us is not an acceptable part in the eyes of others, we will have to choose between honoring ourselves and honoring the values of those around us. But, when we are ready to own our relationship to that piece, to be the authority in our own lives of what is acceptable and what is not, then we can see that we ourselves are the ones to lift that curse. It is then that we can say to that part of us, "I love and accept you fully, just as you are." This is a true answer to the Calls to Wholeness.

URGES

Urges—we all experience them and they can be very powerful at times. Ask any grocer about why they put candy by the checkouts. An urge is a desire without breath. It is a focus on one pleasure or feeling state to the exclusion of all others.

We might say that urges are desires without context. It is I-want-that-now thinking that does not include consequences or other desires. Like a spoiled child, they demand instant attention. But urges can tell us a lot about what it is that we really want. Usually they are spontaneous, not restrained by concepts of "good and bad," "right and wrong," or even what is possible.

Approaching urges from the perspective of something useful being said to us by our body-mind, we can ask ourselves, "What is it that I really want?" An urge for some chocolate may be a desire for comfort or pain relief. An urge to go shopping may be a deep desire to get some respite from difficult problems that need solving. An urge to go to some exotic place may well be a desire to stop enduring our current routine of drudgery.

Another aspect of urges is that they open a window into the strength of what we are suppressing. Urges can be like seismographs; they can show us the magnitude and depth of what we have buried. And because of their spontaneity we can get a glimpse of hidden parts of our being without our usual filters or blinders.

I find it is a great mistake to dismiss urges and righteously change our focus back to the tasks at hand. These urges, too, are Calls to Wholeness. They are messages about how we can return home to ourselves. We don't have to act directly on them. But if we notice what they are really about, we can make wiser choices about our lives.

LUST AND FORBIDDEN DESIRE

Lust is a very strong desire, usually of a sexual nature. Because it is such a powerful desire, it often totally overshadows the other desires we might have that would compete with that lust. For instance, if I were to find a particular woman so desirable that, "I simply must have her!" I might ignore my promises of fidelity to my spouse. That is simple enough and is usually the kind of experience that leads to wisdom about that kind of lust and where it might take me.

What makes lust so tricky is when it is forbidden. That is, when obtaining what we desire is out of the question. We can't have it. But we want it, badly! Annngh! The fact that we can't have it makes the desire much stronger.

What we often forget is that fulfilling desires in the physical reality is not the only way to end the tension of desire. First, we take responsibility for our feelings and recognize that it is our choice to not physically fulfill that desire. In the case of lusting after that woman above, if I will unashamedly and fully feel that desire for sex with her, savor every touch and sensation in my imagination, I can have the *feelings* of my desires being met and leave her virtue (if you will) untouched.

We do this in our sleep all the time. We get to experience these things through our dreams and that's how it's done. The trick, of course, is to be okay with that lust (giving ourselves permission to feel it in its entirety) and to be aware that there are other desires worth fulfilling in the physical world that are very important to us as well; desires which make it worthwhile to just dream the lust and let it go at that.

When we can give ourselves permission to explore ourselves completely, and accept that we will not be damned for our lusts, we can enjoy them without hurting anyone, especially ourselves. Forbidding lust in our hearts makes for an unnatural stress that serves no one. It is like making a big effort to clamp down on the lid of a pot that's boiling over, when all that's needed is to take the pot off the fire. We feel what we feel and then move on.

THE BLESSING OF DISSATISFACTION

"The little dissatisfaction which every artist feels at the completion of a work forms the germ of a new work."
—Berthold Auerbach

One of the precursors to desire is dissatisfaction. We all experience it many times a day. We taste our food and adjust the levels of salt and pepper because we are mildly dissatisfied with the levels of those condiments as presented to us. We roll over in bed because we no longer fully enjoy the previous position. We change the channel on our television sets because we have become dissatisfied with the current station. These are trivial dissatisfactions, but ones surrounding our jobs, our relationships, or our living spaces are very similar, only larger. Dissatisfactions of any size lead to desires. And it is what we do at this point that determines whether we utilize our dissatisfactions or let them go to waste.

For one thing, dissatisfaction puts us in touch with our inner guidance system, the one that shows us when we are in alignment with the deepest parts of ourselves and when we are out of alignment. When we are feeling dissatisfied, then we know that we are being urged towards finding something else that will suit us, in our totality, better. If, for instance, we like drinking a lot of alcohol because we enjoy the effects of inebriation, at some point the pleasure of that inebriation will diminish to the point where there is increasing dissatisfaction. This can best occur when there is little interference by ideas and judgments of what should or should not be done. It is a process of self-aware-ness and needs its own space to develop. I'm speaking here, both from personal experience and my observation of others, about the process of understanding ourselves and growing through the experiences of life. Relationships, jobs, living situations, and appearance can all go through this process of doing something long enough to fully develop dissatisfaction.

There was a certain period in my life when I smoked a lot of cigarettes. I was thoroughly addicted to nicotine. Sometimes I smoked unfiltered Camels, sometimes the French Gauloises (a rough, pungent cigarette, now gone). Both were very powerful nicotine dispensers. Sometimes I used snuff, the "smoke-less tobacco." And sometimes I both smoked and used snuff simultaneously! Nobody's scare tactics had any effect on me. Lung cancer seemed beyond remote and I could put up with the smell, so why couldn't everyone else!

However, the time came when it just didn't make me feel as good as I wanted. In fact, the cigarettes were making me feel less good by making it harder to breathe. Plus, I was getting nastier and longer-last-ing colds. The pleasure level was definitely going down.

Just the same, my body wanted that nicotine hit. And bigger hits to boot. So, in order to make a change, I found that I had to up the dissatisfaction level to motivate myself to quit. I smoked even more than I had been smoking. I took even more snuff. I even closed myself off in rooms so that I could be in the smoke even without a cigarette burning. Finally, the day arrived when I was so fed up with tobacco that I just had to quit. And once I did, it was an enormous pleasure to breathe fully and enjoy the fresh air. Eventually, I could smell the subtest fragrances again and the pleasures of breathing and smelling have been increasing ever since. Thank you, dissatisfaction!

> *"The chemistry of dissatisfaction is as the chemistry of some marvelously potent tar. In it are the building stones of explosives, stimulants, poisons, opiates, perfumes, and stenches."*
> —Eric Hoffer

Dissatisfaction can empower us. By acknowledging that we don't have to endure, that complaining may get us only sympathy or miserable company, and that validation of one's ideas about reality is a paltry pleasure, we move into a position to change things dramatically.

It is the first step in reclaiming our core being. It is the statement that "this isn't good enough for me!" When we can say that, then we are ready to look around for what might be good enough. We start to become connoisseurs of life, seeking out the things that excite us, bring us joy, spark delight, and magically entrance us. Our choices, the options that our minds present us with, become based on what would please us the most, not on what will relieve our fears the most.

It all begins when we honor our dissatisfaction and let it motivate our desire to live and feel even better than ever before!

THE DESIRE FOR MYSTICAL UNION

> *"The finest emotion of which we are capable is the mystic emotion."*
> —Albert Einstein

Feeling pleasure, feeling present, and feeling connected to something greater than our conscious minds are all perspectives or degrees of the same experience. When we talk about Calls to Wholeness we are referencing that experience of being consciously and fully connected to our Higher Mind, Core, Source, All-That-Is, God, etc. This is the mystical union that is so highly prized by seekers of all spiritual paths.

This book is not primarily about attaining that state of bliss. But the skills of pleasure will take us a long way down that road. If we want to feel good, we need to practice feeling good. If we want to feel great, then we need to practice feeling great!

PRACTICE FEELING GOOD

Here's a little exercise to work on that. No matter where you are right now there must be some things around you that you like. Most of us have chosen to be where we are and we have surrounded ourselves with things that bring us pleasure. But even if you are in circumstances that are not of your choosing, there are likely to be things in your vision that you like. So find ten things that you can see from where you are right now that please you. And as you look at them, or hear them or smell them, find within yourself the delight you get when you focus on them. Feel the pleasure and enjoyment of each of these things for at least a few moments. And then savor the whole experience for a while. This is a valuable practice to do every day.

> "Desire exists in you as in every thing. Realize that it also resides in objects and in all that the mind can grasp. Then, discovering the universality of desire, enter its radiant space."
> —Vijnana-Bhairava Tantra

❖ EXPLORING DESIRE ❖

Desires have many levels to them. We may desire a car, because we desire mobility, because we desire freedom, because we desire a deeper connection to the divine. Pick a desire of yours and see if you can find deeper levels to your desire. You might want to repeatedly ask yourself, "At a deeper level, what do I really want?"

We've looked at the nature of pleasure, the principles of pleasure, and now the nature and function of desire. Now we're ready to explore what it is that we can do to expertly expand our experience of pleasure. We're ready to dive into the Skills of Pleasure themselves. These are skills that we can use every day to easily increase the joy in our lives and the overall sense of wellbeing we crave. The first skill is that of Awareness, the foundation of all growth and wisdom.

SECTION II

THE SKILLS OF PLEASURE

Pleasure is always nice, but there are things we can do to have more of it and to make it even better. This is the heart of the book. Here we go over each of the seven Skills of Pleasure and how they fit together as a whole system.

"Ah, mastery…what a profoundly satisfying feeling when one finally gets on top of a new set of skills…and then sees the light under the new door those skills can open, even as another door is closing."
—Gail Sheehy

CHAPTER 4

Skill #1: Awareness

*"If we could see the miracle of a single flower clearly,
our whole life would change."*
—The Buddha

Of all the things we are paying attention to during the course of our day, one of the most neglected usually is just how we are feeling. This is particularly sad when we consider that most of what we are doing is in some way connected to our drive to feel good. Without taking the time to focus on how we are feeling in the moment, we simply can't find out whether we're happy or not, and which parts of our lives are working well for us, and which are not. I think that when we do look, we generally find that we are not as happy as we would like to be. So, if we want to be happy and feel good, we have to monitor those feelings so we can improve them.

Thus, the first skill of pleasure is to be aware of our sense of pain and pleasure. We don't need to wait until an experience gets to an intensity that we just can't help but feel the pain, or only realize the great pleasure we've just had when we look back on it. By allowing ourselves to monitor our pleasure and pain levels closely, we can see ourselves in the moment, experience ourselves in that moment, and make the little course corrections that are needed, as we would in driving a car.

This chapter is about the awareness of our feelings on different levels. This is a two-fold process: being present to our feelings in the moment, and then noting the source of those feelings. We'll look at the different kind of feelings, their relationship to thoughts, our own authentic feelings versus ones we've adopted, and, most importantly, how we feel about how we're feeling.

BEING PRESENT TO OUR FEELINGS

"The struggle of the male to learn to listen to and respect his own intuitive, inner prompting is the greatest challenge of all. His conditioning has been so powerful that it has all but destroyed his ability to be self-aware."
—Herb Goldberg

We start with being aware of all that we are experiencing in any given moment. This is sometimes called "mindfulness" and it develops with being able to simply stay present to what is happening both around us and within us. We do this without making any effort to fit everything into a story of some sort, as though we had to tell someone about it immediately. We simply just pay attention to whatever is there besides what we are thinking. For many of us this is a challenging practice in and of itself.

Awareness of something without defining it or describing it in relation to other things we know allows us to enjoy it for its own sake. This presence to our own experience feels good all by itself. If we become aware of other pleasurable feelings somewhere in our being, all the better.

THOUGHTS AND FEELINGS

The second part of this skill is being aware of where our feelings are coming from. What has brought these feelings up to our attention?

What is going on around us that is related to what we are feeling? What does what we are focusing on have to do with what we are feeling?

Most of us have a great many thoughts going on all the time and we are generally unaware that there are feelings attached to those thoughts. In fact, most of what we feel is directly related to what we are thinking. This is particularly true of thoughts that seem to linger and play over and over.

Let's take an example: we see a naked person. That is an experience. We can then say that nakedness is shameful and feel disgusted accordingly. Or we can say the nakedness is a natural part of life and not give it any more thought. We might even celebrate that person's freedom and feel joyous. Or we can say that nakedness is naughty and perhaps feel an erotic charge from it. Whatever it is that we feel, it is a function of the thoughts and beliefs we have around the intrinsically neutral experience of seeing a naked person.

Each of the reactions we have to our daily experiences is molded by our beliefs about how things "should" be in our reality. If we are law-abiding citizens, then we tend to judge other people on the basis of how well they stay within the law in what they do. If we are rebels, we might judge people in just the opposite way. And there are feelings we get when we approve or disapprove of how other people act. If we choose to feel better, then we can choose the thoughts that will produce those better feelings.

"Tension is who you think you should be. Relaxation is who you are."
—Chinese Proverb

When we are asked about how we are feeling today, very rarely do we inquire of ourselves more than at the most superficial of levels, usually just enough to answer the question. But what happens when we keep going deeper with the question: How do I really feel? It's not a question about our feelings *about* something; it's about what are we experiencing within ourselves right now.

We may not be aware of any emotions at all. Or we may encounter either numbness or some resistance to feeling one or more emotions.

For many, there is a reasonable fear that if I open up to all the emotional "stuff" in there, I may feel a lot of pain that I won't know how to deal with. Feeling all of that may also cripple my ability to get anything done. Fortunately, the "stuff" is mostly there because we haven't accepted something about ourselves and that can change once we give ourselves permission to feel it and see it differently. The rest of the "stuff" doesn't have to be dealt with immediately, anyway. In fact, it usually only comes into focus when we're capable of dealing with it.

"People usually consider walking on water or in thin air a miracle. But I think the real miracle is not to walk either on water or in thin air, but to walk on earth. Every day we are engaged in a miracle which we don't even recognize: a blue sky, white clouds, green leaves, the black, curious eyes of a child—our own two eyes. All is a miracle."
—Thich Nhat Hanh

SPIRITUAL FEELINGS

What are we feeling spiritually? This may be a difficult question if we do not identify with spirit in some fashion. I use the word "spiritual" or "spirit" to denote that part of our experience that seems to be different from physical, mental, or emotional experiences. I am not suggesting that there is an inherent religious, metaphysical, or mystical aspect to these words, although some might want to add those meanings. And feeling into spirit is not as wild as some might think. It is simply becoming aware of oneself and allowing that awareness to extend beyond the body and mind.

We don't have good language for this common experience, but most people connect it with something much greater than our physical selves, either in concept—Creator, Infinite Intelligence, or Divinity—or by observation – the Universe, the Earth, or Nature. Spirit then is that part of our self that experiences things like beauty and harmony, oneness and ecstasy. Just as we know emotions only by our experience of them, we know spirit only by our experience of it.

Our beliefs about those experiences, however, are not the same as reality. They are only beliefs about reality. We constantly work with models of reality; we make assumptions about the nature of the reality that we observe. But these concepts and assumptions, as useful as they may be, are distinctly different from the direct experience of reality and life itself.

So, when we look to see how we are feeling spiritually, we are checking in with our sense of connection to the greater realities. Am I feeling a part of the Universe or am I feeling quite alone and useless? Do I trust that I am loved or am I feeling afraid that I won't ever be loved? Do I see beauty all around me or is my focus on the things that need to get done? Can I find some peace when I feel into myself or is there only chaos inside? Whatever answers we get to questions like this are not only perfectly valid, but they are each a step towards a greater awareness, and thus they are steps towards our greater happiness.

"How alive am I feeling?" This question takes into account several levels of experience at once. It relates to how open or closed we are feeling towards life. It is akin to asking, "Am I ready for Life?" It is also parallel to asking, "How do I feel erotically?" I am using Eros here in a way that is more than just sexual. It is about the free flow of Life energy, call it what you will – prana, chi, ki, orgone energy, odic force, aka, etc. It also relates to how safe we feel, how well nourished we are feeling, and how loved we feel. But more than that, it relates to how aligned we feel to our core, our inner self, our "soul," if you will.

Remember, we don't want to involve judgment with these answers at this point. We may find that we are not feeling particularly alive at all. Okay, that's fine. If we decide that we want to feel more alive as soon as possible, that's fine too. That is something to work on, an impulse to create a different experience. But noticing how we feel right now is what is important here.

PAYING ATTENTION

In all of these feelings there are a number of aspects to pay attention to. How intense are these feelings? Are we feeling more than one feeling at a time? Is there any resistance to our feelings? These resistances usually involve feelings of tension and often have a mental picture that comes with them. We just want to note these tensions and pictures. There's plenty of time to do something with them later. And often these tensions simply disappear when we fully look at them and relax.

There is no utility in thinking or saying, "I shouldn't be thinking these thoughts" or "I shouldn't be feeling these feelings." We *are* thinking and feeling these things. This is our present moment and we don't have to believe that there is anything wrong with this moment.

You are alive and living on this Earth right now and you are what you are. Your experiences right now are just that, your experiences. Judging what you are experiencing is making yourself wrong in every moment. It doesn't make any sense. If you are feeling angry, fine that's your feeling. It is neither right nor wrong. What you do, what action you take in connection with that feeling is another matter. I am simply encouraging you to just look at your feelings without adding meaning or judgment to them. I know this is easy to say and harder to do. But the effort is well worth it.

> *"What is necessary to change a person is to change*
> *his awareness of himself."*
> —Abraham Maslow

Many people have difficulty trying to pay attention to what they are feeling without getting lost in their own thoughts. In fact, it's not at all uncommon for some people to have a hard time even distinguishing between thoughts and feelings. It's like the old joke about the wife who asks her husband what he is feeling, and he replies with what he's thinking. Not everyone is prepared to see his or her feelings on command. One of the harshest criticisms I've seen around encouraging someone to look at what they're feeling is the admonition to, "Get out of your Head!!!" It's a very counterproductive command, because it usually provokes strong feelings of shame and frustration. Thus, it chases away any motivation to feel anything.

But, the art of feeling starts with anything, awareness of any sensation at all. Even an awareness of numbness is a beginning. Awareness is simply paying attention to the experience of the moment. So, if that experience is only around the thoughts swirling around in the head, that's genuine awareness. *Seeing what's going on in oneself, whatever it is, is the foundation for building a life of pleasure and happiness.*

As we progress into the skill of the awareness of our feelings, we find ourselves in recognizable feelings "states." These are more than momentary feelings; they are experienced as going on for a while. Feeling states last long enough for us to enjoy and savor if they are pleasurable, and long enough to loathe if they are not. Typically they are called positive if they feel "good" and negative if they feel "bad." Positive ones include feeling free, in love, satisfied, safe, personally important, turned-on, excited, and happy. Negative ones include fear, anger, hurt, disappointment, disgust, boredom, and sadness. It is these feeling states that become recognizable as patterns in our lives. I find that it's useful to pay attention to our feeling patterns, being mindful that these patterns can always change. How we change these patterns and cultivate the ones we want is the subject of much of the rest of this book.

WHOSE FEELING IS THIS, ANYWAY?

A word needs to be said here about noticing the difference between our genuine feelings and those that we have been taught to have. For instance, many of us have been taught to feel guilty when we desire something fattening, like chocolate cake, particularly if we have been told that we should lose weight. Some people have been taught to feel disgust when they see people with different sexual preferences. And still others have been taught to feel superior to people of different colors, races, or religions.

> *"You've Got To Be Taught To Be Afraid*
> *Of People Whose Eyes Are Oddly Made,*
> *And People Whose Skin Is A Diff'rent Shade,*
> *You've Got To Be Carefully Taught."*
> —Lt. Cable in the musical *South Pacific*, Rodgers and Hammerstein

Unless we take the time to look at the value judgments we have adopted from our families, schools, friends, and the media, we are likely operating on the basis of someone else's feelings. However natural and normal they seem, as familiar as our toothbrush or our favorite slippers, they may not really be working for us.

We will never be happy feeling other people's feelings. They can never be expressing our own Soul. They are simply scripts that we've learned to use in specific situations. If we are to keep moving along on the adventure of pleasure, then we need to be aware of both what we are genuinely feeling and the learned feelings, the scripts that we default to. Our genuine feelings may coincide with the feelings of others, but it only works if our feelings originate within us.

"I pay no attention whatever to anybody's praise or blame.
I simply follow my own feelings."
—Wolfgang Amadeus Mozart

Generally, we can let go of learned feelings once we have spotted them by deciding then and there whether we resonate with them or not. It's like a bit of computer programming that is either allowed to remain in the program or it's simply to be discarded. But we have to actually see it clearly in order to do something about it. We have to be mindful of it. It also requires us to be willing to take charge of how we are feeling and to be the authority in our own lives. We are the ones who have both the freedom and the power to change our thoughts and feelings, and thus to change our lives.

PRESENT FEELING, PAST FEELINGS

Another piece here worth noticing is the difference between what we are feeling in the present moment and what we remember feeling sometime previously. The classic feud is a good example of this. "We have always felt animosity towards those others and so we will continue to feel that now." That may be more extreme than most of us feel on a regular basis, but little things like "I don't like peas" based on a childhood memory of nasty canned peas, or "I don't like the color purple" based on an unfortunate institutional décor, rob us of our immediate feelings.

Taking the time to notice the difference between a habitual feeling, one that is based on the memory of past feelings, and the feeling in a present experience can be very helpful. I recently was confronted with my own prejudice towards peanut butter. I like peanuts but have had a notion that I don't like peanut butter. At some point in my childhood I think I ate so much that I got a little sick. I stopped eating it from then on. A friend gave me some recently and I reluctantly tried it again and, of course, I liked it. Now, I have a new memory of liking peanut butter that is replacing the older memory and I have increased my range of pleasure.

Sometimes when we become aware of feelings, those feelings seem so intense that we feel overwhelmed. We will deal with intensity later on in this book, but for right now it's sufficient to say that feelings of overwhelm don't have to be scary. Very often we feel something like "if I let this feeling in any more I will explode!" We probably won't explode, or die, or be consumed by fire, or anything else dire. We will simply feel more. And, in fact, by allowing a little more feeling in, we expand our capacity for feeling in general, and that includes an expanded capacity for love and joy. That's a pretty nice reward for going a little past our sense of being overwhelmed. Too much of that feeling may well shut us down, but the tipping point can change with intention.

In my classes I talk about the supremacy of experience. By that I mean that what we are actually experiencing in the moment is much more valuable and ultimately much more deeply pleasurable than all of the meanings we make to put it into context. Pleasure doesn't mean anything. Pleasure is simply an experience and that is enough. Simply be aware of what you are feeling, and I'll bet you will feel more alive when you do.

A MODEL SCAN

"The mind's first step to self-awareness must be through the body."
—George Sheehan

So let's put all this together and see what a model scan might look like. I will lay it out in the form of questions, but that's only to make sure we don't miss anything. Once you've done this once or twice, you will probably find that it comes on without much thought at all.

- *What am I feeling in my body?* It's usually easier, at least at first, to close our eyes and go from one end to the other seeing what bodily experiences we notice. What qualities do we notice? That is, is there pleasure or pain? Are there other sensations such as pressure, tightness, numbness, hot or cold? Nothing needs to be done about the things we notice. The simple act of awareness is enough.
- *What am I feeling in my body in the way of energies or feelings?* Are there any emotions that I am aware of? Am I feeling any erotic charge? Am I aware of more than one feeling? Are my feelings changing as I look at them? Where in my body am I feeling these feelings the most?
- *What am I thinking?* Do these thoughts have feelings connected to them? Do I have a sense of frustration or of lingering unsolved problems? Or do I have a sense of accomplishment and competence? Are there any thoughts of desires that are noticeable?
- *How connected to the world around me do I feel?* Do I feel alone or a part of things and people? How alive do I feel? How much joy do I feel? How much love do I feel? Is there any sense of connection to Higher Mind and how does that feel?

Sometimes in scanning our feelings we come across self-destructive or painful feelings and desires. While this book is about becoming skilled at pleasure, we can't do that when we are primarily feeling miserable. There are many techniques for relieving painful emotions. Since emotions generally follow thoughts, an examination of our thoughts, particularly ones involving fear, will usually reveal what it is we are afraid of. And if we look at the deepest level of that fear, it will often be revealed to be a fear of a feeling that we have been avoiding for a long time, like thoughts surrounding self-worth and lovability.

If we think of feelings as energy with information moving in our bodies then we can notice the information, as in "I feel so ashamed that I want to hurt myself."

❖ RELAX AWAY THE PAIN ❖

When a thought gives rise to a pain, shame, hurt, or fear we can often do something about it. Here is a little technique that usually helps. Pay attention to the place in the body where you mostly feel the pain or other sensation and then simply relax that part of the body as fully as possible. Then think the thought again that gave rise to the feeling and check the body. Generally the bodily sensation is reduced or simply gone. We are retraining our bodies to react to the thought differently, without tension or pain. Sometimes we notice that a feeling like that pops up somewhere else in the body. Repeating the process, but relaxing the muscles in the new area, usually does the trick. No technique works every time for everything, and it may take a few rounds to get through all the layers, but for a simple technique this can seem miraculous.

How Do You Feel About How You Are Feeling?

"Everything is perfect in the universe—even your desire to improve it."
—Wayne Dyer

One of the key pieces to becoming skilled at feeling good is being aware of how you feel about how you feel. That is to say, are you happy with your emotional state or not? Are you content to feel just as good as you do right now for a long time to come? Certainly, we want to appreciate the joy we are feeling when that happens. And we want to savor our excitement in those special moments. But overall, is this enough?

What I'm suggesting here is that there is often a nagging feeling that gets overlooked that says that something is missing, something inside is not being satisfied. This is an important awareness because it calls us to continue our exploration of what it means to feel good.

I used to live in the U.S. Virgin Islands, one of the beautiful places on Earth. I was aware of how much I enjoyed being there; I loved the sun, the ocean, the lifestyle. But, there was always a feeling, hidden well below the surface, which was one of dissatisfaction. My life there just wasn't good enough! I was aware of both the pleasures of the moment as well as some feeling that was pushing me forward.

It is this feeling of present discontent, concurrent with many other feelings, that is so valuable. When we pay attention to this feeling, we become more attuned to what is happening at our deepest levels. This is the foundation of our inner guidance system. The more we are aware of these feelings, the easier it is to be aware of just how aligned we are with our core self.

❖ PRACTICING SKILL # 1: ❖
I AM AWARE OF WHAT I AM FEELING.

This simple little exercise can be done in any position at all as long as you can see something. Pick something to look at that is sufficiently small to be essentially a point or dot. Now keep your attention on that spot as best you can and continue doing this for a minute or more. Most likely when you're done, your thoughts will have calmed down some and you have become somewhat aware of what you are feeling. If you want to take this a step further, you can keep your eyes focused on your spot, but now allow your attention to gradually expand out from your spot to include ever-increasing circles of awareness. Do this, with your eyes still on the one spot, until you are aware of everything in your sight, including all the way out to the sides and up and down. Do you like how you are feeling at this point?

Most of us hold ourselves back and limit our lives to the boxes we are most familiar with. What it takes to grow beyond our boxes is both an awareness of what we're experiencing right now, and our own personal authorization to go into unexplored territory. We are being called to be happier and more joyful, but we need to respond and be okay with that greater sense of being alive. That's the Skill of Permission.

CHAPTER 5

Skill #2: Permission

"The more pleasure you can give yourself, the more pleasure you can give to another. Likewise, if you give yourself the pleasure of power, you have more power to share with others. The same is true of fame, wealth, glory, success, or anything else which makes you feel good. And by the way, I think it's time we looked at why a certain thing does make you feel good. Feeling good is the soul's way of shouting, This is who I am! Have you ever been in a classroom where the teacher was taking attendance—calling the roll—and when your name was called you had to say 'here'? Well, 'feeling good' is the soul's way of saying 'here!'"
—Neale Donald Walsch, *Conversations with God*

Have you ever had the experience of having a stranger or acquaintance offer you something that looked appealing, perhaps a bit of food or some help, and because you didn't quite trust them, or yourself, you refused? Have you ever wanted to do something but didn't because you were afraid of what other people might think or say? Have you ever wanted something but hesitated because you felt unworthy of it?

It's very ironic that most of us crave pleasure intensely, and at the same time hold ourselves back, for one reason or another, from enjoying what we have. Why is it that we gobble down a tasty meal, hurry through sweet sex, or do chores as we listen to beautiful music? It's as though we think that the pleasurable things are nice, but not if they get in the way of more pressing things.

It's not enough to just want something in order to bring it into our life. We need to feel that it is okay for us to have it. In order to choose pleasure, to choose to enjoy a bagel, a relationship, life, anything, we must find a way to get past our internal guardians. These guardians are our beliefs about what is proper, appropriate, right, safe, okay, just, reasonable, logical, sensible, and all the other rules we have about how life is to be lived. If we disobey the guardians, we create an internal conflict that spoils whatever pleasure we may be after. So like a teenager who wants to use the family car for the evening, getting permission to do so will make life a whole lot easier.

This chapter is about what keeps us from giving ourselves permission and what it takes to get it. We will look at selfishness, shame, and judgments. We will look at some practical ways to find out the source of our resistance. But most of all, we will look at what it takes to give ourselves permission to be who we are.

"Give yourself permission to get the most out of your life.
If you're spending all your time scrubbing corners with a toothbrush,
you're kind of missing the point. Taking shortcuts doesn't mean
shortcutting the end result."

—Sandra Lee

AM I BEING SELFISH?

When I talk about pleasure, I often see people stiffen slightly and their energy and enthusiasm diminish a bit. While not wanting to openly disagree with me, they gingerly express their objection that perhaps pleasure is "selfish." We all have seen plenty of examples of people who focus only on themselves, and either pay no attention to others or are even mean and rude.

There are many ways we can look at these people we call "self-ish," people who don't act the way we would, or would like to think we would. However, we have no real idea of what inner experiences they are having. The decisions they make may well be the very best ones they know how to make in order to take care of themselves.

More to the point, when we are afraid of being "selfish," we are expressing a fear of what others might think of us. We certainly don't want others to think of us in the same terms we think of those strange people we call "selfish." It is our own judgment coming back around to bite us. We don't want to be the object of the judgments we so easily make about others.

"Giving yourself some loving attention is not selfish. It is sensible. If you feel loved and cherished—even if it is only by yourself—then you will have more love to give to others, too."

—Penelope Quest

Another presentation of this thinking is: "Isn't it selfish of me to put so much attention on my own desires when so many people in the world are suffering?" There are two separate ideas here. The first idea is that it is part of my responsibility to help others. That caring for others is part of my spiritual duty. That my attention to myself detracts from efforts I might make on behalf of others.

You may believe that you have certain spiritual duties in life, but it is your choice to believe that. And if you choose to operate on the basis of duty, then you are coming from a place of concepts of what is right and wrong. Doing your duty, however that is envisioned, is right; not doing your duty is wrong. To help others on the basis of duty can be a pleasure, the pleasure of doing what you are supposed to do. But, it is a far cry from helping others on the basis of love and compassion, where it is a pleasure to be of service. In this place of serving out of pleasure, we can give freely because it feels good to do it. It is a much more powerful, not to mention delicious, way of living than the mea-ger feelings of doing one's duty.

"It is pleasure that lurks in the practice of every one of your virtues. Man performs actions because they are good for him, and when they are good for other people as well they are thought virtuous: if he finds pleasure in helping others he is benevolent; if he finds pleasure in working for society he is public-spirited; but it is for your private pleasure that you give twopence to a beggar as much as it is for my private pleasure that I drink another whiskey and soda. I, less of a humbug than you, neither applaud myself for my pleasure nor demand your admiration."

—W. Somerset Maugham

The second idea in this arena is that it is somehow wrong, unjust, or immoral to be feeling this good when others can't. Extending this logic looks something like this: that in order for me to restore some level of fairness, and since others aren't in a position to enjoy life as much as I do, I must not enjoy my life so much. If I decrease my pleasure, it will somehow lessen someone else's misery. This is obviously absurd. Isn't it true that what we really want is to have everyone enjoying life at least as much as we do? By enjoying our lives *and* doing what we can to help others to enjoy theirs, we can increase the general happiness in the world.

Caring for other people, helping them in small or large ways, is one of the great pleasures of life. When we are motivated by the pleasure of love, we can do great things and we help bring more pleasure into many lives. We are then sharing the joy and excitement of life. But, when we try to do things for others because of ideas of how things *should* be and how we *should* be, we are not coming from our hearts; we are coming from our minds. And when we ignore what our bodies and emotions are asking of us, we create an internal struggle. What we end up sharing is not joy, but conflict. To be happy in "selflessness," we must first find the pleasure in it and then what we have to give is a measure of happiness.

"A selfless act out of even the purest desire to do for others, will be selfish in the satisfaction and happiness it brings to one doing it."

—Ashly Lorenzana

Giving ourselves permission to take care of ourselves in the midst of others' needs can be challenging. Yet, it is the only genuine way we have of increasing the overall joy in the world.

RECEIVING PLEASURE

When I have classes that involve paying attention to one's own feelings, particularly when people are both giving and receiving massage or loving touch, I often hear that it was much easier to give the touch than to receive it. Opening the channel for good things to come into our lives is a critical step in creating a happy life. And, one of the key elements of that is to give ourselves permission to enjoy and to fully feel the pleasure.

The first step in giving ourselves permission to feel pleasure is to work through in our own heads that it's genuinely okay for us to feel good. This conversation within allows us to logically deal with all the subconscious objections to our happiness. Subconscious beliefs such as "I don't deserve to be happy," and "It's man's nature to suffer," don't have a rational basis; they are assumptions that need to be challenged. The subconscious works very logically and many beliefs can be changed by simply pointing out, sometimes repeatedly, that the old belief is neither true nor useful.

"To be nobody-but-yourself in a world which is doing its best night and day, to make you everybody else—means to fight the hardest battle which any human being can fight; and never stop fighting."
—E. E. Cummings

In some ways the permission that we give to ourselves to receive pleasure is more of a claiming. I claim the right to enjoy my life. Every independence movement claims the right to be free. Every artist claims the right to express him or herself as they see fit. The psychological process of individuation is a process of claiming autonomy for oneself. Claiming for oneself the natural right to experience the pleasure of life has nothing to do with other people and their ideas of how to behave.

It is about saying to oneself, "I have the right to fully feel joy and to be happy."

Here's a fun little exercise to try. The next time you're with someone with whom you can be intimate, at least to some degree, try the Three-Minute Game. This is all about permission.

❖ THE THREE-MINUTE GAME ❖

Person A says to Person B, "What would you like me to do to or for you for three minutes?" Whatever Person B comes up with must be agreeable to Person A. Once each side has given their permission for the action, then Person A fulfills Person B's request. This can be just as intimate as both people like, but it doesn't have to be highly erotic. It could simply be a shoulder or foot massage, or three minutes of kind words and compliments. The point is that Person B is receiving what he or she has asked for. Person B is strongly encouraged to give permission to him or herself to receive what it is that they want. Their whole focus for those three minutes should be on the pleasure that they are being given.

When those three minutes are up, and some gratitude expressed, then Person B says to Person A, "What would you like me to do to or for you for three minutes?" And so, the favor is returned in the same manner.

After each person has received, then it's time to go on to the second question. Taking turns again, they ask the question, "What would you like to do to or for me for three minutes?" Again, this can be anything that is mutually agreed to.

This brings in the question of giving another person permission to play with you for a short time. It is also a way of giving yourself permission to let go of control and experiment with surrender. Whatever is done here needs to be negotiated, but this is where many forms of permission are played out.

There is internal permission to ask for what we want, to be open to someone else's desires, to receive pleasure without needing to reciprocate immediately, and to focus entirely on oneself for a time. There is permission to focus entirely on someone else without fear of criticism, to express our own desires about touching or doing something for another without shame, and to be fully present to another as they express themselves.

Of course, three minutes can be extended by mutual agreement to however long you like. But the important thing to remember is that you are both giving permission to another to express and fulfill their desires as well as giving permission to yourself for fulfilling your own desires. Doing this in pairs within a group is also a great social icebreaker.

UNCOVERING OUR RESISTANCE TO PERMISSION

When we discover that we are resisting pleasure in some way, when we find that we're holding back for some reason, there is a set of four questions that we can ask ourselves that may shed light on why we are pinching off our pleasure. The trick to these questions is to ask them in a quiet space and to feel into the answer. The mind's job here is to ask the questions, to focus on what's going on, while the body feels for tightening or clenching. This clenching is the resistance and is a sure sign of some thought that is getting in the way of enjoyment.

1) *Do I have the right to feel this pleasure?* You can change the wording to reflect the specific pleasure you have in mind, but this is the general format. This is about feeling into the sense of appropriateness, or deservedness, or a general sense of okayness involved with the proposed pleasurable event. If you feel some tightness somewhere in your body, you know that some part of you is saying "No." If you then ask yourself "Well, why not?" you will usually get some indication as to the nature of this resistance, as in "I'm not supposed to" or "That's bad." You will then have to decide whether or not you will honor and keep that old belief and, if not, what you will replace that old belief with.

For instance, you may be drawn to sleeping with someone you've only recently met. You ask the question: "Do I have the right to sleep with this person?" And suppose you get a knot in your stomach, what then? Listen to the thoughts that accompany your feelings. Are they thoughts of commitment to another partner? Perhaps, they are thoughts of what "good" people should do. Perhaps they are thoughts connected to a fear of intimacy? Whatever they are, you now have the opportunity to look at those thoughts and to change them to new ones if you wish.

"Poor is the man whose pleasures depend on the permission of another."
—Madonna Ciccone

2) *Do I have the power to do this?* We might modify this to say: Do I have the ability to do this? It's simply a question of looking at all the elements of doing something and seeing if it looks like it can work. In the above example of sleeping with someone, the question could raise issues of physical abilities, logistics, or possibly the fortitude to put up with someone else's disapproval. Whatever it looks like, it is a matter of looking into oneself and asking: "Can I really accomplish this?"

3) *Do I have the will to do this?* We don't really talk about will much in our society. Perhaps we talk about a willful child, one that prefers to do what he wants instead of what we want him to do. But will is essentially intention. It is the part of us that makes things happen. We use our will to get out of bed in the morning and to go off to work. We use it to turn our focus from an exciting game on television to the child beside us who needs our attention. We use our will to demand our rights at City Hall.

In this situation, we are asking if we have the determination to do what it is that we are asking about. It is not about motivation, that's the last question. It's about feeling into ourselves to see if this is something that we can actually put our energies into. In the example of the person we are thinking about sleeping with, the question becomes, "Do I feel I could really follow through with this?"

4) *Do I have the desire?* That is, do I really want to do this? This involves looking at the situation from all the angles we can, to see if at least most of us is on board. In the example above, our body may be very enthusiastic about sleeping with this person, but we may have other feelings as well that aren't so enthusiastic. What then is our overall desire?

Remember that this is about our feelings. We are feeling into the answers to these questions. The thoughts then follow the feelings. We are looking for the thoughts that carry conflicting feelings so that we can decide what we want to do with them.

"As we let our light shine, we unconsciously give other people permission to do the same. As we are liberated from our own fear, our presence actually liberates others."

—Marianne Williamson

HURDLES

As we open to increasingly larger experiences of pleasure, it is common to encounter some resistance within. It's as though our internal guardians say we can only have just so much pleasure. These little hurdles can be somewhat disconcerting and even a bit discouraging. For example, it is not unusual for people participating in workshops that focus on opening the heart and learning to enjoy life more is to feel a powerful letdown soon after leaving the workshop. There is a kind of disbelief that life really could be so wonderful. The same often happens after a vacation.

It is at this time that the skill of permission is needed to counter this rebound effect. Giving ourselves permission to enjoy more, to experience more pleasure is not a one-time deal. Once we have chosen to become more aware of our feelings and to focus on feeling good, all the little beliefs and rules that we have to the contrary start to come up.

It has taken me a long time to get used to the experience of being slightly down and out of sorts after an amazing flight into the realms of ecstasy. While I'm having the great experience, I keep thinking: Well, finally I have gotten into the High Realms of Spirit. Then, I come down into a place that seems like I've taken a step backward and I find myself in some sort of depression that doesn't seem to make any sense. But this is a natural part of the process.

Now I expect this comedown, and don't make too big a deal out of it. I just have to work through all the new thoughts that arise from my depths that challenge my worthiness to these sublime feelings. Once again, I have to give myself permission to feel so good.

PERMISSION TO BE WHO WE ARE

The most fundamental permission we can give ourselves is the permission to be who we are. It is an acknowledgment of our own special uniqueness. It affirms our right to be here on Earth. It recognizes that we are just fine the way we are without having to change for love or approval. And it puts the focus of decisions back on us, as opposed to the choices others might make for us.

"Be who you are and say what you feel, because those who mind don't matter and those who matter don't mind."

—Dr. Seuss

Another way of putting this is: we give ourselves permission to see the world through our own eyes. In order to fit into our society, or any society for that matter, at times we have to be able to see the world through the eyes of others. We need to understand how they view the workings of life and how the society is ordered. Only by having this awareness can we see how we can fit in and be a contributing part of that society. But, that doesn't mean that we want to view the world the way others do all the time. It is like being in a kitchen with family and contributing to a feast like Thanksgiving or a birthday. We likely would make a salad the way most people like it. We probably would grill meat or vegetables in a way agreeable to everybody. But when we are alone we well might make our salads and cook our meat in ways that are very different and much more pleasing to us.

> *"Nothing resembles selfishness more closely than self-respect."*
> —George Sand

If the rules of society are particularly ingrained and we fear being disapproved of for going our own way, then we are trapped. One aspect of learning to enjoy life more thoroughly is to recognize that our pleasures may well not be the same as other people's pleasures. Ultimately, this is tied to our need to give ourselves permission to be fully our own unique selves. Our inner guidance system only works if we are looking inward for our answers rather than outwardly to the guidance of others.

The adage to "follow your heart" is both wise and politically radical. If you "follow your heart" you are not nearly so liable to accept being told what to do, what is important, or what you "should" do. But how do we know we are following our heart? We feel a sense of great warmth and pleasure in that region of the body we call the heart.

> *"Dream and give yourself permission to envision a You*
> *that you choose to be."*
> —Joy Page

In giving ourselves permission to be who we are, we are claiming our own authority. When we take that authority and become the "author" of our own life, we look within and ask questions like: Does this really make sense for me? Does this feel good? Does this feel right? Is there room to doubt the claims of others?

We may well want to believe them, but without some discernment we relinquish our power and the ability to choose our happiness. Even if we choose something that later appears to be less than desirable, we have maintained our authority and learned something valuable to boot. I find that it helps to remember that I'm not trying to make each choice the "correct" one; I'm giving myself permission to explore life, to make "mistakes," and to look for the things that bring me the greatest joy. I claim the authority to be happy.

❖ PRACTICING SKILL #2: ❖
I GIVE MYSELF PERMISSION TO FEEL BETTER THAN I HAVE EVER FELT BEFORE.

They probably don't do this anywhere anymore, but when I was growing up there often were special permission slips that we were given in school that allowed us to be out of class for some reason. It's a useful concept here. Suppose that I give you a permission slip that allows you to do something that you don't feel you can allow yourself to do just now. Maybe my permission slip allows you to take the rest of the week off from work, including housework. Maybe my permission slip allows you to treat yourself extravagantly for one night. Maybe my permission slip lets you to buy something special that excites you.

Whatever it is that you would like my permission for, consider giving yourself a permission slip for that something. Look inside yourself now and feel what it would be like to have permission for that something. Is there some resistance to using that permission slip? If there is, try checking to see if any of the four questions apply: Do I have the right? Do I have the power? Do I have the will? Do I have the desire?

You might want to ask those same questions when it comes to giving yourself permission to be fully who you are.

When we do give ourselves the permission to go into the realms of joy and pleasure beyond what we have ever experienced before, we are treading in territory that can be as foreign as a rainforest jungle or high arctic tundra. We will need not only permission, but also both courage and an attitude that will support that exploration. This is where the Adventurer steps in.

CHAPTER 6

Skill #3: Treating Pleasure as an Adventure

*"The voyage of discovery is not in seeking new landscapes
but in having new eyes."*

—Marcel Proust

It is easy enough to notice pleasurable feelings as they arise. We can appreciate them when they come to us and regret their loss when they're gone. We might call this the "tourist" approach. The tourist is passive; she expects interesting things to happen to her without getting too involved. She goes "sight-seeing." This approach is relatively safe and is filled with things that are to be expected — pleasant comforts, some interesting things "out there," and no particular changes within. But the *great* pleasures of life are not to be found on the tourist itinerary.

It's the adventurer that finds these treasures. She explores and goes to the places the tourists never even know about. The adventurer finds those things that excite, delight, and fill the soul with awe. She experiences things of rare depth and joy, great beauty both inner and outer. And she gets to know herself in the bargain.

Adventure is exploring the unknown in ways that are acceptably risky but essentially fun. A lot of what pleasure consists of is an expansion of who we are. It often involves seeing things in new ways, in opening our minds to new options, in taking roads we've never been on, and in looking to see what's over the next hill. In this sense, growth and pleasure are the same thing, only viewed from different angles. This natural growth may involve some hardship of sorts and perhaps some significant effort, but the sense of personal expansion is usually experienced as exhilarating and fulfilling.

> *"We live in a wonderful world that is full of beauty, charm and adventure. There is no end to the adventures that we can have if only we seek them with our eyes open."*
> —Jawaharlal Nehru

To be adventurous requires a certain degree of self-confidence; it is the willingness to venture into the unknown and to surrender some fraction of control. When we do let go, we open to the world of surprises and, for the most part, it is our attitude towards them that make them pleasurable or not. It's an attitude that says, "Yes, I'm interested in what life has to offer me that I've never seen, what I've never experienced." It's about courageously experimenting with the elements of our existence and seeking new ways to excite our souls.

However, there is more to being an adventurer than enthusiastically charging off to explore the world. Like any skill there a number of components to being an adventurer; elements of consciousness that require focus and practice in order to develop some expertise. Without some proficiency in these components the adventure is likely to be short-lived or only sporadically fun.

FREELY EXPERIMENTING

The essence of adventure is in experiments, those little trials of experience that deepen our understanding of what works for us and what doesn't. There is no reason to think that for some reason we should know everything about the world and ourselves. There is no reason that we should be able to do everything perfectly. We learn by making little and, sometimes, very big trial moves.

"Don't be too timid and squeamish about your actions. All life is an experiment. The more experiments you make the better. What if they are a little coarse, and you may get your coat soiled or torn? What if you do fail, and get fairly rolled in the dirt once or twice? Up again, you shall never be so afraid of a tumble."

—Ralph Waldo Emerson

An important part of this experimentation is playfulness. When we are playful we follow our whims and try out things just for the fun of it. In this way we stimulate our creativity and make a game out of learning. When we experiment we say that we don't know what the results will be. We may have a good idea; perhaps we have a strong preference in how things turn out. The important piece, however, is that we are open to discovery. And in that we open to life.

LETTING GO OF WORRY AND REGRET

Remember that pleasure is only experienced in the present moment. We can only enjoy pleasure, or any of its related forms, when we are firmly focused on the current experience. But, there is something interesting that happens once we have chosen to be happy. Those things that are less than joyous or pleasant become more obvious. We have less tolerance for things that bring our sense of wellbeing down. And two of those things are worry and regret.

Worry is the focus on one or more things that have not yet happened but conceivably could happen. It is the fear that something "bad" might occur. It doesn't matter how remote the possibility of it actually happening, if it exists in the imagination, it has a reality all its own. When worry shows up we usually lose perspective and resonate with some deeper fear within us. It is always about the future and as such it prevents us from enjoying that moment.

I thoroughly enjoy the idea going around now that worry is like praying for what you don't want. It is more deleterious than that, though; worry keeps us out of the creativity that we need for problem solving. It is in a state of pleasure or joy that we are our most creative, and that means being in the present moment. When we relax and feel good, all parts of our mind work in harmony and we can accomplish great things. When we tense up, however, we vastly reduce our abilities. So, not only does worry feel awful, it short-circuits the very inner workings that could help solve the worrisome issue.

When I get overwhelmed with concerns and start to shut down, I generally go straight to a nap. I like naps anyway, but especially when there is "work" to be done. I feel good when I wake up and very often the problems that were worrying me have ready solutions. I have relaxed and given my problem-solving parts the energetic space to do their thing.

Regret and any focus on the past disempower us in the same way. Not only have we abandoned our present experiences, but we are also left unhappy, both about things that have passed and about our own wellbeing. We are telling ourselves a story that things are not as they should be.

For the adventurer, staying present means that she is always open to whatever is happening and is about to happen. Letting go of worry and regret lets her be ready for whatever pleasures are around the corner. The essence of this skill is to pay attention to what we are paying attention to. The more our attention strays to what we don't feel good about, the less joy we can hold.

EXPECTATIONS

> *"High expectations are the key to everything."*
> —Sam Walton

> *"Expectation is the root of all heartache."*
> —William Shakespeare

One of the greatest challenges on the path to greater pleasure, joy, and happiness is mastering expectations. There is a great deal of confusion about what expectations really are, how to use them, and above all how not to be hurt by them. As the two quotes above demonstrate, very thoughtful people can have quite contrary views on these everyday experiences.

Expectations are very curious creatures. We create them all the time but, once created they take on a life of their own. We expect that when we are driving, the road will continue over the hill; we expect that the food in the supermarket won't make us sick; we expect our parents to tell us the truth. And generally we get what we expect. But every now and again something very different happens from what we expect and it shocks us. How could he/she/they/it do this to me? This isn't what I expected at all!!! It's as though there has been a breach of contract, an unspoken deal has been broken. We get upset as though we have been personally attacked.

Expectations are not future reality. They are not contracts with the Universe. They are not something outside of us that is a part of nature. They are simply beliefs we have accepted about the future. Very often our expectations are based on what we think are probable outcomes, on the projection of patterns we see, or simply on the basis of hope and dreams. Sometimes we base our expectations on what other people have said or what we thought they said. Or our expectations are based on meanings we have created to make sense of our immediate world. But, however they come to be, we are the ones who create them. Whether consciously or not, we choose these beliefs and they are our creation. And, like Frankenstein's monster, they can lead to unpredictable, and perhaps, disastrous results when we are not fully conscious of our creations.

For instance, perhaps I love my son so much that I want him to do well in school so that he can go on to a good college. As I envision his great success in life, I create an expectation that he will study hard, get good grades, and go on to a good college. However, if he should find that what he really wants to do is spend his time surfing and hanging with his friends, I may be very disappointed. I might be so disappointed that I withhold love to a large degree to show my disappointment and disapproval. And in so doing I end up poisoning my relationship with this son I love so much. My son is only following his own joy. I am reacting to my own expectations with anger, and doing harm to both of us.

Once I have recognized that I am responsible for my expectations and that they are only beliefs, not some form of reality, then I am in the position to process those feelings of disappointment (and perhaps feelings from the memory of similar situations.) If I created my expectation based on my understanding of how the universe works, my disappointment may well leave me confused. The most useful response is to search for a deeper understanding of the ways of the world so that my new experience can be integrated into my world-view.

If my disappointment is in the actions or non-actions of other people then I have to recognize that there is another factor involved here as well. While expectation is very powerful, it is not as powerful as free will. We can't get people to do what we want with simple expectation. Sometimes, we might be able to manipulate them with shame, guilt, or bribes. But their free will can always override any of our notions of expecting them to do something. They may not even be aware of our expectations about them. To get upset about their failure to live up to our expectations is a form of self-torture. The sanest way to deal with this is to give people permission to be who they are and to do what they do, just as we give ourselves permission to be who we are and to do what we do.

"I do my thing and you do yours. I am not in this world to live up to your expectations, and you are not in this world to live up to mine. You are you and I am I, and if by chance we find each other, then it is beautiful. If not, it can't be helped."
—The Gestalt Prayer, Fritz Perls

Another variant of this is when our dreams become expectations. This can happen anytime but is often found in budding relationships. One person will become so excited about finding their dream mate that they pay less attention to the real person and focus more on who they want this person to be. They project qualities and attributes onto their new love that have much more to do with their own heart's desires than the wonderful, but probably different, qualities of this other person.

Inevitably, the time comes when the dreamer finds out that the other person doesn't actually live up to their expectations. This often leads to a great, but unnecessary, sense of pain. When we that sense of pain comes up, we need to ask ourselves, what expectations have we created about our new love? We do not have to torture ourselves by being disappointed that someone else has not met standards that we have created and which they are probably totally unaware of. A simple understanding of the difference between a dream expectation that we ourselves create and a strong desire for what we want can alleviate the confusion in the dreamer. Expecting the dream to be real is folly. Following our desires and seeing where they lead us is wisdom.

What happens when our expectations, conscious or not, are unfulfilled? This is the source of the disappointment that expectations are so famous for. What we do with that disappointment determines how much pleasure we can have in the ensuing moments. However, most of us seldom look at what disappointment really is. It suddenly comes on us and we experience it as though it is a natural, albeit, unpleasant part of life. It seems to have an overwhelming power to shake us to the core and make us angry at the apparent changes in our world we now have to live with.

But, on closer examination it becomes easy to see that disappointment is really *choosing* to not like something. This is not an insignificant idea. If, at the restaurant, the kitchen is out of what I really want, I have the choice to be unhappy about it or not. I have a great many other ways of responding to the situation, not all of them include feeling bad. In fact, most of them don't. If I claim my power to choose pleasure whenever I can, I probably will choose to order something else and to find another feeling to experience instead of disappointment, and let it go at that!

*"Expecting the world to treat you fairly because you are a
good person is a little like expecting a bull not to attack you
because you are a vegetarian."*
—Dennis Wholey

Expectations are a form of focus, just as intentions are. However, they are a kind of focus that disallows doubt and that is their great usefulness. Once we have become clear about what our desire is and we have chosen to have that desire met, then we put some effort towards meeting that desire and *expect* to have the desired result. This puts our whole being behind bringing our desire into reality and the expectation is the strongest expression of our will. It is much stronger than hope or optimism. It is a visceral kind of faith that involves the body as well as the heart and mind because it removes room for uncertainty. We often sabotage the creation of what we want by letting our doubts sap our energy. When we allow our focus to be dispersed by questions that start with, "What if…" then some of our energy is dealing with the very opposite of what it is that we desire. Consciously expecting something to come to pass bypasses doubt and channels our energy and our will like a laser beam.

But what happens when even our conscious expectation doesn't come to pass? The first thing to do is to look at what *did* happen. Very often what we find is that we have brought into being "the nearest equivalent" of what we had desired. Restaurants often give us an opportunity to discover new dishes when they are out of the one we initially wanted. By paying attention to the nature of our desire, the feelings that we were looking for, it usually happens that the *feeling* we're seeking is right there.

*"Whatever we expect with confidence becomes our own
self-fulfilling prophecy."*
—Brian Tracy

There are four basic elements of successful (and sane) expecting.

The first is to remember that expectations are related to reality only as tools we can use to influence reality. We don't want to mistake them for reality itself.

Secondly, we make expectations a conscious choice. If we encounter disappointment that gets under our skin, then we know it was an unconscious choice of expectation and that we must not have taken full responsibility for it from the beginning.

Thirdly, we can expect anything we want. There are no limits to what we can imagine, what we can desire, and what we can expect to come to us. We are energizing our desires by our expectations in a very powerful way. There is no reason to hold back on influencing the world to fulfill our desires.

And finally, even with no doubt that our expectation will be fulfilled, it may not happen. Something will happen, though, and by looking at what did happen as the closest thing possible given the current circumstances, we can stay balanced, grateful, and happy.

> *"Nobody succeeds beyond his or her wildest expectations unless he or she begins with some wild expectations."*
> —Ralph Chappell

What about the expectations of others? Most of us know how difficult it can be to encounter the disappointment of other people when we don't meet their expectations. As children most of us were taught that we were not supposed to disappoint other people, particularly our elders. Guilt and shame at the very least were the consequences of this disappointment. This, of course, has left many of us very aware of the expectations of others to the degree that we are afraid to disappoint *anyone*, even if it means sacrificing our own happiness.

Expectations used in this way are a form of control, with the threat implicit or implied. They are intended to override our free will. As we grow into maturity we learn to assert our free will more and more, but the habits of yielding to the expectations of others can be hard to break. It is a major claiming of our freedom when we are willing to disappoint others when their expectations conflict with our own sense of wellbeing. Just as we need to take responsibility for our own expectations, we need to let others take responsibility for theirs.

INTENSITY

> *"Only those who will risk going too far can possibly find out how far one can go."*
> —T.S. Eliot

One of the key elements of being a pleasure adventurer is learning to balance intensity. On the one hand increasing one's tolerance for intensity leads to greater and greater levels of joy and love; however, an intense passion without breath and perspective can lead to obsession and pain. This, perhaps, helps to explain why many of us are uncomfortable or suspicious of intensity, particularly intensity of feelings.

Many of the most wonderful experiences of life are very intense. Love is intense, orgasms are intense, childbirth is intense, spiritual ecstasy is intense. And the more we allow ourselves to feel into these experiences, the more deeply we open to them. Learning to let go and allow the awesome power of wonderful, intense feelings to flow is the path to bliss. It is a practice and a skill to be cultivated.

One interesting feature of intensity is that it can be interpreted as pain, as a neutral experience, or as a pleasure depending on how the person experiencing it decides to describe it. A genuine rollercoaster ride can be any one of the three, so can the first time one goes scuba diving or skydiving. It all depends on how we choose to view it or the level of fear involved. Many times what we call pain can be lessened simply by noting that the experience is not particularly painful, but merely very intense.

In the same vein we can take an intense experience that might be scary for us as in rock climbing or public speaking and reframe it as power — the personal power to meet a big challenge. Rather than letting the intensity overwhelm and incapacitate us, we use it to grow with, to see that we are bigger and more capable than we had thought.

Most of us, out of fear, habit, or training, have an unconscious set point for intensity, above which we feel overwhelmed. Generally, we assume that this is part of our nature and that's just the way we are. But that's not always the case. That set point is the dividing line between our comfort zone and everything else. As we have done many, many times in our youth, we can move beyond the limits of our comfort zones, expand our range of feelings, and create larger and larger arenas of pleasure and joy. But it takes a willingness to take a risk and to be okay with a modest amount of discomfort or disorientation. When we do this, we can adjust our level of acceptable intensity and change our set point.

Of course, some people change their set points gradually downward so that they only can accept smaller and smaller amounts of intensity. But the pleasure adventurer keeps resetting his intensity set point to ever-greater levels in order to experience even more pleasure and joy. The intensity on all levels of activities can bring on wondrous joy and exhilaration. It is that intensity that stimulates the feeling of being alive.

Fun

"People rarely succeed unless they have fun in what they are doing."
—Dale Carnegie

Let's look at what fun really is. For starters, fun is an active form of love. It is a dynamic expression of life. Where savoring is about spending time with our experiences and expanding our awareness, fun is about being so totally in the moment that awareness is very focused.

The word "fun" comes down to us with an original meaning of hoax. However, it fills a need for a word that conveys the sense of feeling good while doing some activity. In our modern usage, there is no purpose to fun other than to have some. Fun is its own end, reward, and justification. It is an experience of delight and joy. Where savoring is a private, inner experience, fun involves some form of interaction with the environment or with other people, real or imagined. And there is often some challenge involved with fun. Fun activities engage and stimulate our body-mind as well as our conscious mind. These activities excite us in some way. They are intriguing.

Fun is an essential part of adventure. Without the playfulness of fun, the adventure would be stiff and uninteresting. For the adventurer, fun is the sense of aliveness in any activity. Like unconditional love, where it is wholly given without judgment or reward, unconditional fun is living without restraint or need for approval. It is the excitement of fully engaging in experience.

For some people there is no better purpose to life than living for the fun of it!

Change

When we consider our lives in the context of change we are presented with two dominant approaches. The more common approach is that, since we don't know what is going to happen we need to protect ourselves as much as possible from unwanted change. We take a defensive posture. The insurance industry is built on "managing risk" in this way. A great many of our building codes, health guidelines, and food regulations are in place "just to be safe." It is an approach that is focused on the future and what might happen sometime later.

The other approach is to view change in a more positive way and regard it more like a dance or a grand escapade. Rather than protecting ourselves from change, we embrace it in such a way that we can change with it, and do so in a way that we prefer. This is an attitude firmly fixed in the present. It is about remembering that nothing will last forever, maybe not even for the rest of the day. It is about enjoying what we have in front of us and using the experiences of the present to shape what happens next, the immediate future.

The two different approaches are based on fear and on pleasure. As we have noted before, fear is always about the future. It is the mindset of "What if...?" Any thinking based on fear and "What if...?" will lead to more of the same. We may feel somewhat better when we lessen our personal fear by having contingencies in place in the event of a realized "What if...?" But that kind of thinking never involves real pleasure or joy. It only leads to more thoughts and feelings based on fear.

In contrast to fear thinking, adventurer thinking or pleasure thinking views change with some excitement. "What are the new possibilities that are arising?" This adventurer thinking is focused on the experiences of life and how we can find more to enjoy. It is about exploring living, not living the safest, most comfortable life possible. It may take some courage to let go of fears of the unknown, but so be it. As Sir Francis Chichester, the first person to sail solo around the world on the Clipper Route, said on completing his historic trip in 1967,

"One does these things because one has a certain nature. One cannot get away from fate. If a person does not fulfill his nature, he will lead a frustrated life and be unhappy. If it involves him in fear he will just have to put up with it."

DANCING WITH THE MYSTERY

"The most beautiful thing we can experience is the mysterious. It is the source of all true art and science. He to whom this emotion is a stranger, who can no longer pause to wonder and stand rapt in awe, is as good as dead: His eyes are closed."

—Albert Einstein

At some point each of us comes to recognize that no matter how much we know, there are vast areas of experience that seem to be beyond knowing. These are the things that feel enormous and that our minds simply can't encompass and yet they are a part of our awareness. Maybe we can catch glimpses of a greater reality or experience perspectives from outside our bodies. Perhaps we feel a connection to some intelligence that is infinitely kind and loving. Perhaps it is a sense of a higher order or place from whence all form arises. However we choose to describe our experience, it generally comes under the label of mystery, or more properly, the Great Mystery.

Curiosity, wonder, and awe are three grades of essentially the same feeling state, which in itself is a form of love. But it's a form of love that has a special interactive quality. There is a sense of engagement with curiosity, wonder, and awe. It's as though a part of our spirit extends out, wraps around, and intertwines with the subject of these feelings. And in return we get filled up and fed by the essence of the subject. It is a connection that is alive and makes us feel even more vital. Curiosity, wonder, and awe are doorways into the Great Mystery.

> *"Sell your cleverness and buy bewilderment."*
> —Rumi

At whatever level we do it, exploring the Great Mystery is a magnificent adventure. We admit we don't know. And we admit that we don't have to know. The exploration is more than seeing new things and answering questions. In fact, the question defines the adventure. The answer only announces that the adventure is over. This is about the experience of connecting to spirit (or God, the Buddha within, Source, etc.) And this experience is almost always incredibly pleasurable. There certainly are painful things that can come up, memories and unfinished feelings usually, but these can be dealt with. What we're playing with here is a good example of how connecting to our deepest parts is a huge pleasure.

One way of looking at the experience of curiosity, wonder, and awe is to see it as a contemplation of ourselves. The subject that inspires these feelings isn't responsible for how we feel. We are dealing with internal affairs entirely. It is the recognition that there is a splendor that we have tapped into and that that splendor cannot be separated from our being. We are an essential element of the Great Mystery. Now there's an awesome thought!

The skill of Treating Pleasure as an Adventure is a big one. As we've seen there is a lot to this skill, as it is comprised of so many smaller skills. But there is no reason to be daunted, because this skill is about stretching our views of who we are wherever we are. It is about being willing to see more than what we currently see. There are no markers that suggest we should be anywhere other than where we are right now. However, there is an invitation here for us: an invitation into the unknown.

❖ PRACTICING SKILL #3: ❖
I AM OPEN TO ADVENTURE AND THE EXPLORATION OF ALL THE PLEASURES OF LIFE.

Think of some adventure that you have been on that you can remember fairly clearly. It could be something that you did physically, something you did intellectually, or even something you did entirely in your imagination. What about it made it seem like an adventure? Was it fun? Was it challenging? What were you exploring? Did you find the adventure satisfying in some way?

Now that we are willing to explore and experiment, it is time to choose what we want to experience, take responsibility for what we are calling into our lives, and make whatever happens work for us. This is the skill of Actively Choosing Pleasure.

CHAPTER 7

Skill #4: Actively Choosing Pleasure

"Be happy in the moment, that's enough.
Each moment is all we need, not more."
—Mother Teresa

The first three skills are about getting ready for pleasure. We clear away all the debris that might get in the way of enjoying ourselves. Then we lay the groundwork by putting ourselves into a frame of mind where we are open to pleasure. And now it is time to start bringing in all the materials for our joy.

The first step is to organize our building blocks. As in most organizational systems we start with what's most important. In this case it's importance itself: choosing what to make important. If we choose to make feeling good important, then we need to recognize that we're the ones who are responsible for our feeling good from beginning to end. Taking that responsibility is key.

Like the different kinds of building materials that go into a structure, when we are interested in actively choosing pleasure, we have many kinds of choices. We are talking about those things that we can do besides recognizing pleasure when we see it. The easiest one is to look for pleasurable aspects in everyday living. Perhaps because it is easy, it is the most often overlooked one. But, it is extremely powerful. Everywhere we look we can find things that can please us. It is not so much that they are inherent beautiful or delightful. It is the attitude we adopt that makes them that way. When we can look out at the world with love and joy, that's what we will see.

The second step takes a little effort but it's clearly worth it: to actively create pleasure. We create pleasure with our imagination, both active and passive, mining our deeper levels for fun and joy. We look for ways to add joy to the world. We can always share in other's joy if we choose to. And we can always do little things with the intention of bringing more pleasure into our lives and the lives of those around us.

And the third is the least obvious and probably the most important: framing our stories in terms of pleasures instead of miseries. We take charge of the meanings we make concerning things, because whatever meanings we make are fundamental to the experiences we have. In order to have experiences we like, we need to frame our existence, the stories we adopt about our personal reality, to be in alignment with what it is that we want.

MAKING PLEASURE IMPORTANT TO YOU

"The mind is its own place, and in itself, can make a heaven of Hell, and a hell of Heaven."

—John Milton

Just how important is pleasure to you? Or to put it a little differently, how important is feeling good to you? I am always surprised, when I ask this question in a group, at the equivocal nature of many of the answers. There is a lot of distrust of pleasure and feeling good out there. As we have said before, we are exquisitely built for pleasure and our primary motivation is to feel better and better. So when we are not so sure about how important pleasure is to us, we are essentially saying that we are not fully comfortable with who we are as human/animal beings. By making pleasure and feeling good a priority, we are affirming our own value and the validity of our bodily existence.

Changing importance levels is a matter of relativity, what's more or less important than something else. It can be as simple as deciding that feeling good is more important than feeling bad. Or it can be spelled out more clearly by choosing pleasure over anxiety, shame, self-righteousness, duty to one's station in life, or what others think about you. If pleasure or feeling good is very important to you, you may decide that getting angry with others takes you away from pleasure so much that it is not worth it. We can change our level of pleasure simply by adjusting the relative importance of things.

I have ruined a number of good dinners at restaurants by being angry at poor service. I finally decided that enjoying my meal was much more important to me than allowing disappointment and resentment to join me at my table. I make it a point now to always be happy with the service no matter how lax it may be. It feels a lot better that way.

This is a great exercise to do in the course of your day, to simply be aware each time a feeling of disgruntlement or judgment comes up and to ask yourself, "How important is this, really?" If you have chosen to make pleasure important to you, I suspect you'll quickly let go of most of those less pleasant thoughts and the feelings that come with them. A few days of this exercise can change your life dramatically.

> *"My life has no purpose, no direction, no aim, no meaning,*
> *and yet I'm happy. I can't figure it out. What am I doing right?"*
> —Charles Schultz

Making pleasure important also gives the body permission to become more sensitive to pleasure. The more attention we pay to pleasure the more deeply aware we become of the exquisite feelings we are experiencing. And the more we are reverberating in pleasure, the more we are broadcasting our feelings to others. Pleasure is contagious. When we uninhibitedly enjoy something the more likely it is that someone else will get a sense of it and want it too. There is a famous line in the movie *When Harry Met Sally...*, spoken by a woman diner sitting nearby Sally (played by Meg Ryan) and Harry (played by Billy Crystal) while Sally is loudly demonstrating her faked orgasms. The other diner enthusiastically says to the waiter, "I'll have what she's having!"

Even a smile is contagious. Have you ever noticed how everyone's mood seems to pick up a bit when a genuinely happy person enters the room? They are people who have said to themselves in some way or another that feeling good is very important and that they choose to experience as much pleasure as they can.

THE MOTHER OF PLEASURE

> *"Most of us can read the writing on the wall; we just assume it's addressed to someone else."*
>
> —Ivern Ball

I think that even the most casual observation will reveal that most of what we experience comes from choices we have made. Either we have made the choices directly, as in deciding what to eat for lunch, or we have chosen to let someone else make decisions for us, as in not voting in elections. Just the same, when we take responsibility for our choices and our actions, we put ourselves in a position of choosing on the basis of something and that something can be pleasure.

When things "happen" to us we have a wide range of choices of ways to react. While most of us have habitual patterns of reactions, those reactions are entirely our choice and thus our responsibility. And again, we can choose to react with pleasure in mind or in some other less pleasurable way.

A friend of mine recently told me of the time when she was driving in Nice, France, down by the waterfront. She's one of those drivers who is constantly jockeying for position in traffic, much to the annoyance of many. She had just pulled in front of a fancy car before stopping at a light when she looked back and saw a hand shoot out of the driver's window and speak to her. As she described it, the hand was very clearly saying to her, with some considerable sarcasm,

"Oh, you go ahead. Be my guest!" She looked again and saw that the eloquent hand belonged to Sean Connery. Mr. Connery had chosen to not get angry but also to not ignore my friend's aggressive driving. He chose to use his considerable skills of expression to say what he needed to say and then to get on with his life. Each of us has thousands of opportunities each day to react to things and to do so with anger, fear, amusement, or pleasure. The responsibility for those choices is ours and ours alone. That's why I say that responsibility is the mother of pleasure.

Responsibility, of course, has many children—happiness, success, and contentment, to name a few. But, taking responsibility for our own pleasure gives us the ability to experience it when we want to, how much we want, with whom we share it, and when to let it go and move on to something else.

A very big part of taking responsibility for our pleasure is also taking responsibility for our levels of stress and tension. It is very easy to say that our stress was caused by such-and-such or so-and-so, but that just leaves the stress stranded in our bodies without a way to move on. However, by first saying something like, "I am tensing up because I am concerned about something," we acknowledge that we are the ones who created the stress we're experiencing. If we created it, we can create its absence. The real opposite of stress is relaxation, and that is *always* a pleasure itself.

> *"God has entrusted me with myself."*
> —Epictetus

So, we are talking about taking responsibility for our relaxation and that's very doable. There are many ways to relax and many good books on how to do it well. However, what is often overlooked is that we stress ourselves when we have some sort of emotional conflict within us. Perhaps we stress because our in-laws are coming and we really don't want to spend time with them, but, at the same time, we don't want to prevent our spouse from enjoying them. Or we stress because of an upcoming exam that we deeply want to pass, but we are afraid we might fail. Sometimes we stress ourselves without knowing why we are tensing up.

By putting the ball in our own court, so to speak, we can intentionally relax those parts that are tense without resorting to outside intervention. We don't need pills or cocktails or something to smoke. We can do it simply with our intention and choose a simple exercise like breathing or visualization. In fact, any attention paid to our bodies will relax us. That is the simplest way to come back into the present and to be with ourselves. Becoming aware of our breath is both very easy and very effective. But a focus on the activities of our left big toe will also relax us. And any pleasurable touch will do the same.

Visualizing something peaceful, like a calm pond or sleeping cat will relax us. So will visualizing something beautiful like a flower or a rainbow. I like to use a mountain stream by a meadow with a great expansive view. The point is to find something that works especially well for you.

Focusing on someone else's healing, "sending" them love and healing energy is a very powerful way of relaxing, as well. It has the same effect as loving yourself, but without any of the possible negative overtones about worthiness and selfishness. It usually comes as a surprise to people when they discover that thoughts about or directed towards others are taken personally by their own bodies. That is to say, that a judgment about someone else's body weight will be taken by your own body-mind as a criticism of you about your weight. A criticism of your neighbor's intelligence will be taken as an evaluation of your own. And conversely, admiration of someone else's skills or beauty will have the same effect on your body-mind as if you had complimented yourself. So, of all the wonderful things to think about someone, including yourself, words of love and feeling good probably have the most magical effect on your own body. Simply blessing and appreciating others and everything around you is a powerful way to relax your body and to energize it at the same time. I highly recommend giving this a try.

"The best years of your life are the ones in which you decide your problems are your own. You do not blame them on your mother, the ecology, or the president. You realize that you control your own destiny."
—Albert Ellis

As you become your own authority, your body-mind will increasingly look to you for guidance instead of outside somewhere. A gentle but firm command to "Relax" any particular muscle group is likely to have an immediate effect.

Looking for Pleasurable Aspects in Everyday Living

"A person will be just about as happy as they make up their minds to be."
—Abraham Lincoln

Once you have chosen to make pleasure important in your life and you have taken responsibility for the pleasure you take in life, then it is simply a matter of looking for pleasure in all that you do. We all notice what we're looking for much more than if we're focused on something else. So it's not surprising that we see pleasure more when we are looking for it. What is surprising is how much more pleasure we find when we become attuned to it. For instance, when we are looking for beauty it is not just that we become aware of more beautiful things, ordinary things become more beautiful to us. When we are looking for kindness or brief interpersonal connections in our daily interactions, we don't just become more acutely aware of them, we start creating them. Just by having an interest in these small charms we seem to bring them into being.

"Make up your mind to be happy. Learn to find pleasure in simple things."
—Robert Louis Stevenson

We can find something to enjoy in just about every situation. I'm not suggesting that anyone should ignore the painful parts of life, or that difficulties should be ignored in favor of a focus on some immediate pleasure. Taking care of these things is usually the quickest way back to a state of feeling good. What I am suggesting is that keeping our energy or vibration up, even in the midst of turmoil, by paying at least some attention to the things that are enjoyable helps to keep us in the present, out of fear, anger, doubt, and stress. As I have said before, being aware of some pleasure is one of the quickest ways to get centered in our bodies, and it is in that space that we can act with our whole being.

It's like the old Buddhist story of the man who was being chased by a ferocious tiger. As the tiger got right behind him his only hope was to jump off a cliff. Part way down he was able to grab onto a branch of a tree growing on the side of the cliff. He looked down and saw another tiger with an equal interest in him as dinner. Out of the corner of his eye he spotted a strawberry growing right there. In spite of what likely awaited him he grabbed the strawberry and ate it. It was the sweetest strawberry he had ever eaten. And in those "ordinary" moments that make up most of our existence, there are hundreds of big and small delights to be enjoyed, if only we choose to look for them and choose to enjoy them.

THE STORIES WE TELL OURSELVES

"All that we are is the result of what we have thought. The mind is everything. What we think, we become."
—Maharishi Mahesh Yogi

Very often we encounter situations in our lives where we have a choice as to how we classify them. If I get to the Post Office and there is a long line, I can choose to become angry that part of my day is being wasted standing around. Or I can take pleasure in having a few moments to relax and perhaps chat with neighbors I've never met. If I find that I'm eating a dish that is a little spicier than I'm used to, I can immediately proclaim that the dish is too d***** hot and refuse to eat it. Or I can say that the experience of eating this dish is more intense than usual, but still quite delicious.

"The truth is that we can learn to condition our minds, bodies, and emotions to link pain or pleasure to whatever we choose. By changing what we link pain and pleasure to, we will instantly change our behaviors."

—Anthony Robbins

The idea of perfection is a good example of the power of how we frame our experiences. Many of us are always looking for perfection in how we look, how we live, even how we make love. We see something that is nice but rather than focusing on what we like about it or what is already great about it, we look for how it could be improved. We overlook the many ways that we could be enjoying this thing or situation and instead put our attention on what doesn't please us. There is nothing wrong in looking to improve something. It is a natural part of our creativity. But what often happens is that a situation or object is compared to how we think something *should* be. What we have done here is to negate the pleasure of the moment. We cheat ourselves of the opportunity for great pleasure in what is already present. There is plenty of time for creating another moment of pleasure that differs in some way from the present one. Both moments can be filled with delight instead of ruining one for the possibility of enjoying the other.

"When you're passionate about something, you want it to be all it can be. But in the endgame of life, I fundamentally believe the key to happiness is letting go of that idea of perfection."

—Debra Messing

Perfection is an attempt to control the world and limit its randomness and change. When we chase after perfection for its own sake we lose our sense of what supposedly makes something "perfect," that is, its beauty or pleasure-giving qualities. Without its grounding in pleasure, perfection makes no sense. To take the pleasure out of perfection is like taking the rubber away from a balloon, there's nothing left but an empty concept. And when we leave the pleasure in perfection, then everything is perfect in the moment of its enjoyment.

Frankly, I'm always amazed at how changing one little bit of a personal story can change everything. I was speaking with someone recently who told me she was really irritated with a coworker who had intentionally snubbed her by not inviting her to a particular party. I was really surprised at how upset she was. When I told her that the party was for those born in the sign of Aries, she quickly forgave her coworker and went happily about her work. Her feelings changed the very instant the story she was telling herself changed!

The stories we tell ourselves and to others about our past are collections of recollections strung together with some meaning that we have chosen that helps us have a sense of order. We may not like that order, but at least some part of our experience makes sense.

"If you keep telling the same sad small story, you will keep living the same sad small life."

—Jean Houston

However, let's look a little deeper into these stories. For one thing, any story we tell filters out most of the details of what actually happened. We aren't even aware of most of the actions, colors, clothes, sounds, smells, and plants around us at the time. What we remember are aspects of the story that affected us emotionally the most. Usually we remember most vividly our reactions to what happened. If, for instance, we were abused by some trusted person as a child, we're likely to remember the feelings of outrage, shame, or a sense of betrayal. We take the bare essentials of the story, so-and-so used his hands in ways that I didn't like, and flesh the story out with adverbs and adjectives that convey the feelings we experienced. While the abuser did things that were unacceptable to us, and probably to society as well, they were not responsible for how we chose to react to those events.

We may choose to tell our stories in a particular way in order to affect others who hear us. We may have been taught that when something like this happens, this is how we tell that story. People react to experiences differently largely by the way they frame the story about it. For those who tell a story of abuse in terms of how terrible it was will feel terrible. For those who frame the story in some wider context that, while not condoning it, can make sense of it as something that does not have to ruin a life, they can move on to more pleasant things.

"Those times of depression tell you that it's either time to get out of the story you're in and move into a new story, or that you're in the right story but there's some piece of it you are not living out."
—Carol S. Pearson

The first thing to remember in situations like this is that the story we tell is not reality itself. It has a lot to do with actual experiences, but it also has large elements of the storyteller's art. Focusing on the things that don't feel good can distort the memory and make the past seem to be only bad. It's rare for anyone to have only bad things happen for their entire childhood and youth. Most people have a variety of experiences that affected them in various ways. Secondly, if we are serious about wanting to feel as good as possible as often as possible, then we want to choose a story that adequately explains the events but leaves us feeling as empowered as possible. To do that, we eliminate as many words of victimhood as we can. We look for perspectives that keep us centered. And we allow our compassion to be expressed where appropriate, especially towards ourselves.

Fear-based Thinking Versus Pleasure-based Thinking

"Fear is the path to the dark side. Fear leads to anger. Anger leads to hate. Hate leads to suffering."
—Yoda

The difference between fear-based thinking and pleasure-based thinking is that fear-based thinking is predicated on the assumption that the world is a dangerous place. For most people this assumption is simply immutable fact. They would tell you that this is the nature of the world and that you'd better get used to it if you're going to survive. But that's only an assumption, a way of looking at our experiences.

Let's see what happens if we hold a different assumption. We might say that this is a beautiful world that works as hard as it can to make our lives as joyous as possible. All we have to do is stop resisting the love and abundance. We might recognize that there are challenges to be met, difficulties that force us to change our plans, and circumstances that change who we are. But we can still look out into the world with joy in our hearts instead of fear.

Perhaps you are saying right about now, "That's nice, but what about all the crime in my neighborhood, all the terrorists that want to blow me up, and then there's my cheating lover? Where's the pleasure here?" I would say to you that you are experiencing fear right now because of the way you are thinking and what you are focusing on. If you were to relax, look around at all the beauty that surrounds you, think of the things you enjoy, and remember the family and friends who love you, your thoughts would be different.

From that different perspective you could see that whatever crime you have in your neighborhood is either worth doing something about, annoying but not worth moving for, or that it's time to go elsewhere. You have the choice to find a way to return to joy and pleasure. The risk of getting hit by a car, or even getting hit by lightning, is much greater than getting blown up by a terrorist. Allowing your focus to stay in a place of fear takes you out of perspective and, as a by-product makes you more miserable. And if your lover is cheating on you, you need to ask a few questions. Is this cheating worth dissolving our relationship over? What is my part in this scenario? What would I like to do now that would make me feel better? Anger and hate probably aren't on that list.

> *"Happiness is something that you are*
> *and it comes from the way you think."*
> —Wayne Dyer

Fear-based thinking thrives on feelings of powerlessness. These feelings naturally come with thoughts that there's nothing I can do about what I don't like. But that's never true. You always have things that you can do to make yourself feel better. Suppose that you have just lost your job and you have no other source of income. Since you got depressed about losing your job, you were no fun and your lover left you. And since you had no more money, you couldn't buy the medicine you need to stay healthy. Naturally you're pretty miserable and worried about becoming even more miserable. Let's start by remembering that we generally see what we expect to see. If we are feeling miserable everything around us appears to reinforce that view.

However, when we intentionally start to feel pleasure, even if it's just little things like noticing children laughing, remembering someone we care about, dreaming of a full belly and satisfying work, we start to see things that are in alignment with our thinking. Opportunities become more obvious and our demeanor is more inviting to potentially helpful people. Our subconscious starts working in ways to support that new thinking by remembering things that we did that were successful. Our conscious minds, no longer encumbered by depressing thoughts, are now free to imagine solutions to our problems. Our entire being thrives and works to bring us back to health and happiness when we return to a state of pleasure and joy. What we need to remember, and sometimes we need help in remembering, is that we have the power to change our thoughts and feelings. It may take some practice, but we can do it. And, ultimately, we are the only ones who can do it.

Sometimes our fears are so intense that nothing will get rid of them until we face them completely. It's at times like this that we allow ourselves to imagine what would happen if the worst comes to be. When we can do this and feel some acceptance, then our fears dissipate and the creative parts of our minds function again to find ways of solving our problems. This takes a little courage, so we need to be gentle with ourselves. But I think that Robert Frost had it right: *The best way out is always through.* We march on in the face of all those things that scare us until, almost magically, we arrive in an emotional place where the fears have fallen away and we can see clearly again.

Another factor in the fear versus pleasure thinking is that the imagination, so necessary in problem solving, works much better when the body is relaxed and having fun. Solutions and alternative possibilities come much more easily when the mind and the subconscious body-mind are excited. Abraham Maslow talked about this condition as the Flow State. It is that place in our selves where we can let go and allow our deepest creativity to run freely.

Choosing to make our decisions from the perspective of pleasure is a big part of this skill. It requires some shift in the thinking patterns for most of us. It adds another layer of complexity to already complex situations. There is no suggestion here that it will always be easy to move from a fear-based thought pattern to a pleasure-based thought pattern. But the change in habit will definitely be worth it.

THE GREATER PLEASURE THEORY

While many people use it all the time, fear is actually a poor motivator. Fear imagines pains, and sometimes those imagined pains are much greater than the real pains could ever actually be. But even these exaggerated fears often don't motivate us to change our behavior much.

However, pleasure, of one sort or another, is consistently a good motivator. So the Greater Pleasure Theory states:

If you wish to change a behavior, find a new behavior that promises even greater pleasure than the old behavior. Thus, if you wish to stop smoking, rather than scaring yourself with horrifying pictures of lung disease, find a pleasure in not smoking that is greater than the pleasure of smoking. For me, it was enjoying the pleasure of breathing easily and fully, something I paid attention to every time the thought of a cigarette arose. Others may find a different pleasure, but the point is the same. We move naturally towards pleasure, so we take advantage of that and find pleasures that work for our whole being that are consistent with our nature.

❖ PRACTICING SKILL #4: ❖
I CHOOSE TO FIND THE PLEASURE IN ALL THINGS.

For one whole minute, look at all the things you like about yourself. Repeat things, if you need to. Then, for one minute look at all the things you like in your environment. Finally, for one minute, look at all the things you like about life. How do you feel right now? We can feel good anytime we want to, simply by shifting our focus like this.

Once we have clearly chosen to seek out feelings that please and nurture us, we still need to be able to take advantage of them. We might well ask, "These feelings are nice. Now what? What do I do with them?" And that's where the Skill of Savoring comes in.

CHAPTER 8

Skill #5: Savoring

"You'll seldom experience regret for anything that you've done. It is what you haven't done that will torment you. The message, therefore, is clear. Do it! Develop an appreciation for the present moment. Seize every second of your life and savor it. Value your present moments. Using them up in any self-defeating ways means you've lost then forever."

—Wayne Dyer

If the essence of pleasure is to enjoy the moment then it's clear that one of the ways to have more pleasure is to string more moments of enjoyment together. That's the art of savoring. Savoring allows us to build upon the previous moment's pleasure and thus to be present to an even greater pleasure. In addition the experience of savoring is often one of becoming aware of pleasurable feelings beyond the point of the initial pleasure. When we savor something we really like, then that sense of pleasure and wellbeing can spread throughout our whole body.

This is the difference between taking a bite of good ice cream on a hot day and saying that this is good versus relaxing into the pleasure of that bite of ice cream and letting the sense of total enjoyment fill our entire being.

Savoring is an appreciation of the present moment. We can be experiencing our memories with pleasure. But that is a present-time experience of remembering. We can experience great pleasure as we contemplate the future, but that is also a present-time experience of imagination. Savoring is both an experience of presence and one of focus. We savor by focusing on the feelings we are having in the present moment.

In this chapter we will explore the major aspects of savoring as well as some of the great kinds of savoring, like beholding, gratitude, and intimacy. And it is here that we can study with one of the truly great teachers of savoring—chocolate.

THE FOUR MAJOR ASPECTS OF SAVORING

"He who distinguishes the true savor of his food can never be a glutton; he who does not cannot be otherwise."
—Henry David Thoreau

The first aspect is to simply spend time with the object of savoring. I like to say that time is pleasure's best friend. When we take the time to fully enjoy something, we let the sense of feeling good sink in. We allow ourselves to relax into the delicious sensations at hand. It is in these moments that we can feel our aliveness. It is a time when we feel okay to open up to a little more of life. We can take in a little more of the beauty and joy that is around us.

The second aspect is to be aware of experiencing pleasure. This is an appreciation of oneself in the midst of pleasure. It is an acceptance of the pleasure one is having and allowing that pleasure to continue. It is devoid of questions about the propriety of the pleasure or any time constraints. It is simply saying, "Right here, right now, I feel good!" This often evokes the response of "mmmmmmm!" I believe there is a correlation between the "mmm" sound that ends such mantras as OM and the natural expression of pleasure that is "mmmmmmm!" Both are instinctive vocalizations of joy, the one about inner pleasures of connecting with the divine, and the other about more sensual outer pleasures.

The third aspect of savoring is to reflect on the experience of the object and to be aware of the fullness and complexities of the experience. It is an act of contemplation that allows as many factors as possible to be absorbed at once. The wine connoisseur does this when he contemplates the various flavors he tastes in a single sip of wine. One can savor music, art, a beautiful car, or anything else in the same way.

And the fourth way is to expand the context of the experience to include a comparison to other similar experiences, as in: "This is one of the best tangerines I've ever had." We do this naturally by associating the current experience with other similar ones. Taking the time to savor gives us the opportunity to also enjoy the memories of other pleasures as well.

BEHOLDING

"A fool bolts pleasure, then complains of moral indigestion."
—Minna Antrim

There is no place to go with savoring, nothing to accomplish. Savoring is both the activity and the reward. It is of value all by itself. It is an act of beholding where one sees what it is and takes it in without any need to do anything about it. To see a beautiful person and just admire their beauty is beholding. It is an awareness that one is feeling particularly good about something but that nothing else need be involved.

Beholding is important because it shows us a different way to deal with desire. For instance, seeing a beautiful piece of art, the newest electronic marvel, or some divine clothing often provokes something like, "Oh, I absolutely must have that!" There is an urgency in this that involves a notion that I can't be happy until I get this; a sense that something needs to be fulfilled; that the moment is insufficient in itself. When we do this we are both forfeiting the present pleasure and tensing up in our compulsion to force the future.

When we allow ourselves to simply behold something, we relax the need to own it and we can enjoy it in the present moment. Beholding is to be present to ourselves as we encounter something that stimulates us. Of course, there are many things that stimulate and motivate us into action. But there is always a trade off: either behold and let the future take care of itself or let go of the present pleasure and go to work to create a situation with a potential for greater pleasure.

> *"We become what we behold. We shape our tools*
> *and then our tools shape us."*
> —Marshall McLuhan

The art of beholding begins by taking a deep breath and savoring the moment without any agenda. It involves an honoring of the beheld, an appreciation of the beauty, sexiness, grandeur, or simple magnificence of it. It involves an honoring of the feelings we are having at the moment. For some people this can be a little tough; the power and intensity of the feelings may seem to demand a successful resolution involving possession of some sort. However, for those skilled at beholding there can be great delight in the moment, taken deeply and slowly, followed perhaps by action, but not necessarily. The enjoyment of the moment is the entirety of the treasure.

Beholding also gives us the breathing room to pay attention to our pleasure on all levels. If it is a beautiful person that we are beholding, we might feel physical arousal, a sense of emotional love, admiration for their beauty, and a sense of connection to the angelic realms, all at the same time. And in so doing we get to customize our pleasure by what areas of our pleasure we choose to focus on. A big payoff for not trying to do anything!

GRATITUDE IS A FORM OF SAVORING

> *"We can only be said to be alive in those moments when our hearts*
> *are conscious of our treasures."*
> —Thornton Wilder

When we say "thank you" for anything, there is an acknowledgement that something pleasant or pleasurable has occurred. It may be fleeting but that moment of appreciation is the recognition of enjoyment.

Gratitude implies that whatever we are grateful for didn't have to happen or be this way. We recognize that things could have been different and that we are glad that they were the way they were. This appreciation adds a great deal to our happiness.

The longer we stay in this state of gratitude, that is, the longer we give ourselves time to savor what we are grateful for, the more deeply we reinforce to our subconscious or body-mind that this is something we like and want more of. As I have pointed out before, a lot of what we bring into our lives is a function of the patterns we have created for ourselves. Gratitude reinforces the patterns we really like.

PASSIVE VERSUS ACTIVE SAVORING

When we are enjoying the aromas of the dinner we're beginning to eat, when we let the flavors of the food fill our mouths, when we feel the textures of the food with our tongue, and experience the satisfaction of the food sliding down our throat, that's passive savoring. It is the immediate awareness of the various pleasures in our senses. It is the basic sense that this stuff is good!

I don't use the word "passive" here in any derogatory way. It only denotes that we don't have to do much of anything except notice whether we experience it as good or not.

Active savoring, on the other hand, is the exploration of the inner territory of feeling. It is a contemplation of the emotional state induced by something, coming back to the original stimulus only as a way of maintaining that state of enjoyment. It involves the third aspect of savoring I mentioned above, that of being conscious of the experience as one is experiencing it. When we use thought to analyze an experience, we involve another arena of pleasure, the mind. When we enjoy our food in good company, we compound the pleasure and involve our hearts as well. When we allow the experience of pleasure to envelop our whole being, we are savoring on a spiritual level. We feel not only the pleasure of the original source, but also a pervasive sense of wellbeing.

Active savoring can take us from enjoying a specific experience to enjoying life in general. It can take us from the pleasure of a certain thing to the pleasure of enjoying our whole existence and it can easily take a person into a kind of trance or bliss state. It's not uncommon for people to go into a reverie listening to great music or smelling an intoxicating fragrance.

Active savoring can be done with any kind of sensory experience as long as there is a great amount of pleasure involved. This is one of the principles of Tantra, that there are many paths to the divine through the senses. The experience doesn't necessarily have to be in a sacred setting. I nearly got thrown out of a barbecue house one time when the waiter didn't understand the bliss I was experiencing with some particularly good ribs, eyes closed and smiling ecstatically. So be forewarned if you're going into that state in public! He probably thought I was on drugs of some sort. But you don't need drugs to get high if you know how to savor!

BODY TIME VERSUS MIND TIME

The conscious mind is fairly good at keeping track of time. As part of its job of being in control of everything it needs to make sure that it knows where it stands in the time order of things. But the body is very different. It understands two things—now and what it is told is real.

There is a famous story of Robert Shackleton, the Antarctic explorer, taking his exhausted men over the mountains of South Georgia Island at the end of an extraordinary row across the frozen Antarctic seas. He allowed them to sleep for ten or fifteen minutes but told them they had slept for several hours. They believed him and kept on going as though they had had a good, long nap.

"The notion of linear time is an objective construction of the human mind, one that is particularly ingrained in the Western attitude toward life. We in the West give more credence to objective, or mechanical, clock time than we do to our inner, subjective time sense. We ultimately reduce all subjective senses of time to the merest thread of objective

agreement. Yet our inner, subjective sense of time is as real as any sense
can be. We think that since we can't measure it, it can't be real. But
what could be more real to us than the innersense of time through
which we experience rhythmic variations like music and even
the pace of our own thoughts and feelings?"

—Fred Alan Wolf

Once some other part of the mind is engaged other than the con-scious in-control mind, the sense of time mostly disappears. Sometimes this sense of timelessness can be dramatic. At the time of orgasm, for instance, both time and space can dissolve into a vast warm emptiness, visions can take place, and a sense of eternity can be felt. We all have had the experience of time "going too fast" when we are enjoying our-selves. "Time flies when you're having fun" is a common expression. But while the body doesn't have a sense of time, the body does take some time to relax. Muscles can relax fairly quickly, but only once they have been told that it is safe to by the control centers of the mind. Savoring gives us the time to let our bodies relax into deep pleasure.

Many of us are addicted to excitement and for us to go into savor mode feels like withdrawal. We feel very alive with excitement and simply do not want to let go of that feeling. But, as wonderful as it is, excitement shuts out or overrides most other feelings. As we let excite-ment subside a whole stream of other feelings can arise, some may be uncomfortable at first. Savoring after excitement is a time when we are very open and aware of our feelings and that makes it a very use-ful time. It is by working through the feelings—sitting with them and feeling them fully—that we prepare ourselves for bigger adventures and higher feeling states.

SAVORING AND INTIMACY

We allow ourselves to savor when we let down our defenses and open up fully to something. With something like chocolate we suspend all judgments about it and simply welcome it unequivocally. We let it into our lives without reservations, as we would embrace a small child.

There is something very intimate about savoring. In fact, savoring is the very essence of intimacy.

Savoring is a form of consciousness and, like all consciousness, it contains an element of self-identity. It is the awareness of an "I-ness" enjoying something. It is self-conscious in the same way that saying, "I love you" is. When we say those words we generally focus on the "love" and the "you." But the message is really something about who I am. I am saying that I am aware of that part of me that *is* Love when I think of you. In the same way, when I am savoring I am aware of a part of me that is pure Joy. And the more I allow myself to focus on that part of me, the more Joy I am aware of and the more comfortable I become with that glorious part of me.

Savoring is part of our primal communication with the world—I like this and I don't like that. Babies know how to savor. As I have watched them, I see that once satiated with milk they hang out in a stupor of savor, savoring the feelings of being nurtured and loved.

> *"Most men pursue pleasure with such breathless haste*
> *that they hurry past it."*
> —Soren Kierkegaard

Savoring our intimacy is the way we recognize ourselves going into the special places of our heart. It is the surest sign that we have opened ourselves to the delights of the universe. When we can allow ourselves the opportunity to speak to the innermost parts of who we are, we see so much joy and love there that the ordinary pleasures of life are paltry in comparison.

Intimacy feels so good because we are inhabiting, without reservation, the basic part of our nature. It is not covered over with thoughts and fears. It is unashamedly naked. It is that place within that feels whole and pure. It is not a foreign space for most of us. We're there when we give to someone we love. We're there when we walk out into a brightly starlit night and feel the awe of infinitude. We're there when we hold a newborn baby of any species and marvel at the glory of life. These are some of the many manifestations of the Heaven within.

The craving for the nurturing feelings of intimacy may spring from the body memories of incubating in our mothers, but now that we're adults we're in no less need of those pleasures. The difference is that now we are the ones who are responsible for providing the nurturing and love we so desire.

Intimacy is the whole enchilada. It is the stripping away of all those things that delude us and keep us from seeing our selves. Intimacy is how we give voice to our inner choir. Without intimacy we wander alone in the world, separated from our cores. Intimacy is not so much about connecting with others as it is about our awareness and expression of our divine core. Savoring keeps that awareness alive so that it can deepen and grow. Savoring feels so good that it makes distractions much less inviting and tempting.

Savoring is a reflexive act; something we do consciously that seems to begin outside of us, but in fact, is about our own being. When we can truly savor ourselves, we have joy and love to give to others. We can only give to others what we have ourselves.

❖ PRACTICING SKILL #5: ❖
I SPEND TIME WITH MY PLEASURES
AND LET THEM FILL MY ENTIRE BEING.

There are many excellent versions of the chocolate meditation, all of which involve extended attention to the experience of tasting and swallowing delicious chocolate. This version does that as well, but adds the dimension of active savoring to the overall experience. It takes the deep awareness of pleasure and allows the savoring to include the dimension of spirit. Here we are encouraged to use the enjoyment of chocolate as a symbol for all the great joys of life and to use it as a bridge to the divine.

We use chocolate in this meditation because it has some unique powers for most people.

Chocolate has the power to center us. As with anything sensual, focusing on the sensations brings us immediately back into the present. With chocolate, our very strong enjoyment of it is a big motivation to stay in the presence of it.

It has the power to delight us. I use the word "delight" to express both feeling good and the stimulation we experience. It is a special kind of aliveness that seems to light us up and make us more willing to see the bright side of things. We experience love, joy, and delight whenever we let go of fear, anger, and doubt. Chocolate lets us do that for a moment. If we do it often enough, we can live most of our lives without those negative feelings.

And it has the power to shift energies. Chocolate has a way of changing both our focus (what we're looking at) and our perspective (what else is included in our field of vision) so that our experience seems to change after eating chocolate. It's as though we have changed the channel that we're watching. Somehow the new channel is a lot more agreeable than the old channel.

> *"Look, there's no metaphysics on earth like chocolates."*
> —Fernando Pessoa

To prepare, you will need chocolate that you can really enjoy. It doesn't matter if it's milk chocolate, dark chocolate, semi-sweet chocolate, or white chocolate. However, most people seem to find that dark chocolate works the best. It has a fuller richness of flavor with fewer other flavors to distract us. The choice, as always, is entirely up to you. It is, after all, your pleasure.

If you do not like chocolate or cannot have it for some reason, any savory tidbit or particularly delicious fruit will do. I've done this for people using candied ginger, mango, even the classic French dish, Steak au Poivre!

❖ THE CHOCOLATE MEDITATION ❖

Take a small piece of the chocolate, hold it in your hands, and give thanks for it. Feel its shape and texture. Then smell it. Take your time and get as much sensory information from it as you can without putting it into your mouth. Note how you feel in anticipation of eating this chocolate.

Let each breath help you to relax into this experience. This is about being as thoroughly in your body as you can, present to all you perceive.

With great consciousness and flair, put the chocolate into your mouth and focus your full attention on the sensations you experience in your mouth. Feel it melt and move around in your mouth. Be aware of the sweetness on your tongue, the creaminess throughout your mouth, and all of the delicious flavors present. Prolong the experience as much as you can while being aware of how it makes you feel emotionally. See how deeply you can enjoy this chocolate.

Now become as exquisitely aware of the feelings of pleasure as you can. Let the chocolate help you hold your attention on the source of the pleasure, but now you want your focus to be on the pleasure itself. Let your experience of pleasure fill your whole body. With each breath let it expand beyond the limits of your body into your whole being. Slowly, breath by breath, let your pleasure fill the whole room. Take your time. Let your pleasure keep on expanding and expanding, all the way out into the universe. Allow yourself to totally enjoy the magnificence of your new expanded pleasure. Give yourself permission to hold this for as long as you want. And when you are ready for this to end, give thanks and reset yourself for new delights.

"Researchers have discovered that chocolate produces some of the same reactions in the brain as marijuana. The researchers also discovered other similarities between the two but can't remember what they are."
—Matt Lauer

As wonderful as savoring chocolate is, it's now time to remember that all pleasures pass. So how do we stay happy when the things that underpin our happiness fade away? That's the subject of the next chapter: the Skill of Letting Go.

CHAPTER 9

Skill #6: Letting Go of Pleasure

"You have to savor special moments like last night, you have to enjoy them, which we did. But it's time to move on now."
—Bruce Bochy

We know that pleasure rises and falls; it builds in intensity, has a crescendo (often glorious), and then declines. Generally pleasures come to an end naturally and we are more or less ready to move on. The end of a meal comes when we are sufficiently satisfied and we don't want to eat any more. Movies are made to end after around two hours because for most people the pleasure declines if the movie goes on much longer. As delightful as sex is, it too comes to an end quite naturally.

But while the pleasure itself declines, the felt memory of the very good time often remains. Quite naturally we want more of those really wonderful feelings. And all too often we make ourselves very unhappy because we can't get back to them. There are also plenty of times when the pleasure ends abruptly and we don't feel we're ready to be done. The Skill of Letting Go is perhaps the hardest one to master. It is about how we say goodbye to what we love.

In this chapter we look at the steps we can take to gracefully move on to a new pleasure as an old one comes to some kind of end. We will also look at some of the things that hold us back from making a nimble transition. It is here that we look at such important sub-skills as forgiveness, forgetting, and understanding change. And most especially we will look at how we can powerfully put gratitude to work for us.

"When one door closes another door opens; but we so often look so long and so regretfully upon the closed door, that we do not see the ones which open for us."
—Alexander Graham Bell

Most of us are taught as children that in growing up we need to learn how to let go of things in order to take care of more important things. We have to go to bed so that we can get enough sleep in order to go to school and learn, etc. We have to stop playing and having fun in order to meet the needs of our parents. We have to stop eating those cookies so that we can save our appetites for dinner. Our parents, or the people in those roles, tell us when pleasure has come to an end and we have no choice but to obey.

However, when we become adults and have the ability to decide for ourselves what to do when pleasures have come to an end, we have a choice. We can rely on rules that we have learned or heard that tell us what we *should* do. Or we can feel into ourselves and use our own inner wisdom. The first one is fairly easy, as long as we can find all the appropriate rules. The second is much harder but leads to a greater exploration of our humanity.

Even knowing that all pleasures must come to an end doesn't always prepare us for the sense of loss we feel when we no longer can enjoy something. The feeling of unhappiness and a mild to severe anger at the thought of the end of that pleasure is a sure sign that we have become emotionally attached to having that pleasure. We take the loss of that pleasure personally; a part of us seems to be threatened. So let's look at what's going on here.

ATTACHMENTS

An attachment is simply an emotional connection to something or someone. We make attachments all the time—in the friends we make, the possessions we like, the activities we care about, and the opinions we form that help us understand our place in the world. The difficulty with attachments and why they are regarded so poorly in some circles comes from the fear of some sort of pain involved with breaking the attachment.

> *"It's not much of a tail, but I'm sort of attached to it."*
> —A.A. Milne, *Winnie-the-Pooh*

Let's take my dog, for example. I am clearly attached to my dog. I feel great joy when she greets me when I come home and I enjoy her companionship. I love her greatly and I don't want to lose her. But not wanting to lose her is a desire to defy the natural laws of change. I know that there will come a time when we must part.

The spiritual philosophies that suggest that it is unwise to become attached to things and people do so with the presumption that you are powerless to avoid feeling the pain that arises when the inevitable loss occurs. Is this kind of suffering really unavoidable?

Suppose that we could learn how to not stay in that pain for long, if at all. Suppose we learned how to handle the end of one pleasure and how to refocus on something new. We would not be afraid of the pain of loss, then, because we had learned the skills of letting go. Most of the time we already do that; we have had enough losses in our lives that we can handle a little more. However, inevitably there come challenges to our abilities to deal with the loss of things to which we have become deeply and thoroughly attached.

The key piece here is developing our ability to handle change. Having found something that brings us a measure of joy, we're understandably reluctant to let that joy go. But situations and circumstances will always change. It's our skill in dealing with that change that makes the difference.

"Life is a series of natural and spontaneous changes. Don't resist them; that only creates sorrow. Let reality be reality. Let things flow naturally forward in whatever way they like."

—Lao Tzu

There are a great many reasons why we might resist change. Sometimes we can't imagine ever being able to be as happy as we have been in the situation now past. I hear things like, "Nobody will ever love me the way Molly did!" or "Nothing can ever take the place of playing the piano for me!" Things have changed without our permission.

Defining and identifying oneself in a particular way can make it difficult to change, as well. For instance, it's not uncommon for one or both people in a relationship to identify with the relationship. Being a part of the relationship, say the Mary of "Bob and Mary," may be a great pleasure to Mary. It becomes a part of who she feels she is. Breaking up with Bob may or may not be painful in itself. But if she has identified with the relationship then she may well experience the pain of losing "part of herself." This is an attachment of identity.

Sometimes we focus so narrowly on one particular thing that is pleasant or fun that we ignore other things that are difficult to deal with. When that one particular thing goes away, we're then left with all the unresolved issues. And sometimes we just get so comfortable that we resist any changes that make us uncomfortable.

Resisting change is usually some form of anger that things have changed. If I am feeling grief about the loss of a loved one, I am angry because that person is no longer there. Sadness is a milder form of grief, but it is still in the realm of an anger that things have changed. Letting go of that anger is a prerequisite for moving on in pleasure. Fortunately, we some good tools to do that: forgiving and forgetting.

FORGIVING AND FORGETTING

Forgiveness, the willingness to not care anymore about some real or perceived assault on our being, no matter how great or small, is useful anytime. If we are keeping ourselves out of happiness because we feel wronged in any way, by some person, some circumstance, or some deity, we are the ones who suffer, not anyone else. When a pleasure ends and somehow our source of joy has disappeared, then it is common to look around and see who's responsible. Someone else may be involved with the source of our joy in the moment, but ultimately, we are responsible for how we feel. By taking responsibility for our own feelings, it becomes quite easy to forgive. Whatever the other person or deity did, they did for their own reasons. But they are not responsible for how we feel about it and it is up to us to react to the new situation in a way that maximizes our pleasure in a fresh way.

> *"To forgive is to set a prisoner free and discover*
> *that the prisoner was you."*
> —Lewis B Smedes

Sometimes getting angry makes us feel a little better. Screaming at the referee who makes a bad call gives us a small sense of power in a powerless situation. But it's a false power, we can't really do anything, and it doesn't get us anywhere. Anger is like taking poison and hoping the other person suffers. Our anger makes us suffer instead. Forgiveness, just letting it go, allows us to regain our place in joy quickly, if that's how we have chosen to live. Forgiveness is a gift we give to ourselves.

> *"To forgive is wisdom, to forget is genius."*
> —Joyce Cary

Many of us think that it is a virtue to remember as much as we can and forget as little as possible. We have systems to help us increase our memories, programs to follow, abundant theories to consider, and condolences and jokes when our memories are not what we think they should be. However, this point of view overlooks the very important role that forgetting plays, not only in everyday life, but also in how we are crafting our lives.

"This kind of forgetting does not erase memory, it lays the emotion surrounding the memory to rest."
—Clarissa Pinkola Estes

Forgetting, even forgetting the things we have enjoyed, is a critical part of life. Some things we may choose to keep in our memory. But we do so at the risk of inhibiting our ability to craft new joys. When everything is fresh and new, we see the beauty more clearly. When our minds are not clouded by judgments, good or bad, we discover the people and things around us with fresh vision. Life is an even greater adventure to those who know how to forget and learn in new ways.

Whatever the change that we are resisting is, and however that resistance came about, we're still faced with some major change in our lives that we don't like. But, like it or not, change will happen. Our happiness doesn't have to disappear when it does, though. If we choose to stay happy, we can.

THE MOMENT OF LETTING GO

"Don't cry because it is over. Smile because it happened."
—Dr. Seuss

I don't think that most of us notice the moment when we go from accepting that one pleasure is finished and we are beginning to be ready for the next one. But I find that moment to be very interesting. We come to a place where we are no longer satisfied with what is. The pleasure may have dissipated so much that it no longer feels particularly good, or we may see an even greater pleasure around the corner, perhaps we are simply ready for something different, or perhaps the focus of our pleasure is simply no longer there. In any case, there is a subtle shift in us. Something inside has pushed us to move on, perhaps reluctantly.

With so many opportunities available, recognized or not, these are the little moments when the choices we have made and the rules we have created about what is possible, and what is not, come into play. How we are crafting our lives reveals itself here. In each of these moments, we reset ourselves, we change the direction of our lives a little. I believe that at these moments we are trying to get a little closer to fulfilling some deeper desire, one that probably has never been voiced, but which has been calling us for a long time. We get closer to fulfilling that deeper desire every time we go from being dissatisfied or sad to something that looks to be more pleasurable. Each time we try to make our lives a little better, each time we pay attention to what we want, we learn a little bit more about ourselves and bring ourselves into alignment with our core being just a little bit more. It is a Call to Wholeness.

GRATITUDE

> *"Gratefulness is the key to a happy life that we hold in our hands, because if we are not grateful, then no matter how much we have we will not be happy—because we will always want to have something else or something more."*
> —David Steindl-Rast

To start the process of letting go, one of the most basic things to do is to simply be grateful for all of the pleasure we have experienced with what it is that we are letting go of. It is quite natural to focus on the sense of loss when a given pleasure comes to an end. But that focus leads to pain. The more we put our energy into feeling unhappy that we no longer have what was previously pleasurable, the more we increase our unhappiness and postpone moving on to something else pleasurable.

However, by putting our focus on giving thanks for what we have received, we can come to terms with the end of this one phase of our lives. This elementary act of gratitude helps to break the sense of attachment we may be carrying. It allows us to look at what is happening from another point of view and frame the situation as one of many wonderful things that happen in our lives. Gratitude comes from a place of greater perspective. It is a perspective that recognizes that there was no inevitability to our specific pleasure. Gratitude lets us remember that these things come and go. When we express our gratitude, when we give thanks, we are saying: It didn't have to be this way, but I'm glad it was! It didn't have to happen, but I'm very happy it did! Gratitude acknowledges that things change and that pleasures do come to an end. It thus allows us to come to terms with the closure of that pleasurable event.

Gratitude allows us to stay in a pleasurable place (remembering our pleasure) while we step back from that pleasure and let it go. It is truly one of the great transition feelings, like anticipation (where we begin feeling good about something that hasn't yet happened) and grief (where we adapt to a major change in our lives.) Sometimes we express our gratitude in advance as in the blessing before a meal. In so doing we are acknowledging several things at once: the pleasure we expect to experience, that this experience didn't have to happen like this (thus the sense of grace or gift), and our understanding that this will come to an end at some point.

"What you focus on expands, and when you focus on the goodness in your life, you create more of it. Opportunities, relationships, even money flowed my way when I learned to be grateful no matter what happened in my life."
—Oprah Winfrey

Gratitude does another thing for us. It acknowledges that we have given ourselves permission to enjoy this experience. It reinforces our confidence that feeling good is not only okay, but is, in fact, good for us. We accept the fulfillment of our desire. Without this sense of the acceptance of our desires and their fulfillment, we undermine our inner motivation to accept any new sources of pleasure. If we don't in some way celebrate the enjoyment of life, why should it matter that new pleasures await us? As we saw in the last chapter, gratitude is a form of savoring and as such it helps us put pleasure into its proper perspective—that it is an essential element in our health and wellbeing.

*"To educate yourself for the feeling of gratitude means to take
nothing for granted, but to always seek out and value the kind
that will stand behind the action. Nothing that is done for you
is a matter of course. Everything originates in a will for the good,
which is directed at you. Train yourself never to put off the word
or action for the expression of gratitude."*

—Albert Schweitzer

THE THREE STAGES OF LETTING GO

One of the key pieces to letting go of pleasure is to admit that those marvelous experiences that we enjoyed so much are over. When we are feeling sad or, more deeply, feeling grief, we are feeling a kind of anger that things have changed when we didn't want them to. Often, we feel that we have been robbed, that there has been a great injustice done, that this just isn't right. And with these thoughts comes the anger that this outrage has happened. However, the longer we hold on to that anger, the longer we get to feel the effects of it. These effects are familiar to all of us—tiredness, mild-to-severe depression, pessimism, etc.

Acknowledging that things have changed is a gift we give to ourselves. It is an act of kindness that soothes our soul even while it opens the door to uncertainty. We know the truth of it but find that truth unpalatable. This is one of those special times when we need to take care of ourselves as we would a sick child. The more tender we can be, the more gentle, caring, and loving, the more effective we will be in the long run.

Not only are we acknowledging that things have changed, but that we have changed as well. The parts of our world that we have cherished are different now. We have come to know a part within us that we love (even though the object of our love may be someone or something outside of us.) Even though we will always be able to cherish the memory this person or thing, it seems as though we've lost part of who we are. It may take a certain amount of courage to face ourselves in the light of this or these changes. But we can do it.

Acknowledging the changes is the magical key that opens other doors to joy. Without that key we are locking ourselves out of our rightful happiness.

So how do we put all of this together to let go of pleasures that have come to an end? I recommend a three-step process: gratitude, acknowledgment of change, and resetting for new pleasures. We've talked about the magic of gratitude and this is the time to invoke it thoroughly. Then, when we feel ready, we say, preferably out loud, that we acknowledge that things have changed. The effect is more powerful when we can physically hear ourselves say what is in our mind.

A sample statement might look like this:

"I give thanks for all the joy I had with (whoever or whatever we are letting go of.) And I know now that things have changed. I now turn my focus towards all the new joys ahead of me."

RESETTING OURSELVES FOR NEW PLEASURES

Gratitude and acknowledgment that things have changed leave us in a place that is perfect for looking forward to the next opportunity for pleasure. By having given ourselves closure on one chapter, we are ready to open a new one. This is the process of resetting ourselves and it is basically a change of focus. When we have that emotional sense of the completion of the last experience, we can look around us, savor what we are experiencing in the present moment, and then move on. We can move back into our adventurer mode to see what else lies out there to discover.

There is nothing wrong with leaving the past behind. It was great (or not), but it's not today. We don't owe the past anything. It is life already lived. Now is the time for new life. If we use The Skills of Pleasure well, we can be confident that the joys to come will be even better than the ones we have experienced so far. Resetting ourselves means relaxing into the openness of infinite possibilities. At some level we are initiating a new adventure. Remembering the pleasures of adventure and joys of new connections helps us to walk away from the past with confidence and hope.

❖ PRACTICING SKILL # 6: ❖
WHEN PLEASURES COME TO AN END
I GRACEFULLY LET GO OF THEM WITH GRATITUDE.

EXPLORING CHANGE

Think of three things that have changed in important ways in your life in the last year. Notice how easy or difficult it was for you to adapt to those changes. Also notice how you are now after experiencing those changes.

Now think of something in your life that is in the process of change right now. It might be something obvious or dramatic, or it could be continuing changes that you are well aware of. Be aware of how you are handling these changes and notice that you are still here and able to enjoy life even as you go through these changes.

And now think of three changes you would like to make in your life. Are there any feelings that you have when you think of the changes you would like to make? Are these feelings all positive, all negative, or a mix of positive and negative?

These little exercises are meant to prepare us for the changes that are inevitable in our lives. Once we get comfortable with change, then letting go of a pleasure that has run its course becomes easier.

Letting go is a precious time. It is a new beginning and, as such, it is a potent time to adjust our lives. Gratitude has been a time of reflection, particularly about those things that we enjoyed. At the resetting time we both remember what we are grateful for and how we might create our lives a little differently. One of the most useful questions that comes at this point is: What desires do I have that have been overlooked or ignored? That is to say: What else is going on inside me? And what parts of me are not enjoying life as they might? That is a large part of what the next chapter is about: Developing a Pleasure Strategy.

CHAPTER 10

Skill #7: Developing a Pleasure Strategy

"To know what you prefer, instead of humbly saying 'Amen' to what the world tells you you ought to prefer, is to keep your soul alive."

—Robert Louis Stevenson

So we've come now to the last of The Skills of Pleasure. We have become aware of what we are feeling and how we feel about that. We have given ourselves permission to feel better than we've ever felt before. We now look on life as a great adventure and we actively choose pleasure whenever we can. We have seated ourselves at the feast of savoring. And we have learned how to let go of pleasures that have come to an end. Now it's time to step back and look at our lives from the perspective of the master craftsman and see how we're doing in terms of creating the lives we truly want to live.

The skill of developing a pleasure strategy is about looking at all the factors that go into giving us pleasure and making some conscious decisions about their relative importance. How do we weigh one pleasure against another? Ultimately, it comes down to how each prospective activity aligns or diverges from our sense of who we are and what it is that we want from this adventure on Earth.

Let's remember that feeling good is the aim of all human endeavors. This good feeling includes all the great joys of service, devotion, kindness, and tenderness. We can be both selfish and generous in the same moment. It follows, then, that the more pleasure that we find or create is for our greater good. It is important both to us and for us. By keeping in mind that feeling good is our priority, we can then choose from a field of options all of which will add in some way to our joy. And we are choosing on the basis of joy, not fear.

IMAGINING GREATER PLEASURES THAN WE HAVE EVER KNOWN

> *"All I want is a room somewhere,*
> *Far away from the cold night air.*
> *With one enormous chair,*
> *Aow, wouldn't it be loverly?*
> *Lots of choc'lates for me to eat,*
> *Lots of coal makin' lots of 'eat.*
> *Warm face, warm 'ands, warm feet,*
> *Aow, wouldn't it be loverly?"*
> —Eliza, from *My Fair Lady*, Alan Jay Lerner

As we develop our pleasure strategy, we envision what it is that we want to experience. To do that we usually rely on the memory of previous experiences. But if we are truly going to go for the very best, the most wonderful pleasures possible, we have to use our imaginations to discover doorways into new and grander pleasures. The process starts by opening to the *possibility* of even greater pleasures. This, in turn, involves resetting our pleasure set points. For instance, I might find that I am comfortable with this much pleasure and joy but more doesn't fit in with my vision of myself.

This is one of the important places where the Skill of Permission comes in. We see these pleasure set points in things like what restaurants people will allow themselves to go to, how much erotic pleasure they can take, and how they envision their ideal life.

Because of these pleasure set points, there is often some tension when we try to exceed our perceived threshold. I remember once when my wife and I had finished a very exciting and heart-opening four-day workshop. It wasn't half an hour after leaving that we got into a horrendous argument. We had exceeded our set points and unconsciously were coming back into a more normal (for us) balance. It wasn't until we recognized what had happened that we could consciously reset ourselves and open to the greater joy that we had so recently found.

It's a wonderful exercise to contemplate joy or love or ecstasy or pleasure and to say to ourselves, what happens when I open to even more of it? How much joy/love/ecstasy/pleasure *can* I experience? And if and when there comes a voice that says something like, "Oh no. You can't go there! That's just too far!", that's our sign that our set point needs to be changed. A gentle but firm, "Oh yes, I can!" perhaps repeated often, is a good start. If we follow that with affirmations that express our heartfelt determination to open to more joy, then we tell our subconscious (where our rules of reality live) that we are serious about how much more we want to experience and that we fully believe that it is possible to experience more.

Another useful exercise is to contemplate our notions of what an ideal afterlife might be like. If you are so inclined, think about heaven, nirvana, or satori. Or, if your ideal state is simply total union with All-That-Is, what would that look like? What would that feel like? You might regard this exercise as getting ready to experience it full time or you may just call it bringing Heaven down here to Earth.

CHOOSING AMONG MANY PLEASURES

As we come to the actual development of a pleasure strategy, we need to be able to contemplate a huge variety of possibilities and levels. The contemplation of all these potential pleasures and joys can be overwhelming. That's why this is a skill, something that we want to get better at, but that takes some time and effort to master. When we do take a good look at what pleasures are most important to us, life gets simpler. By understanding our priorities, we can more easily let the lesser pleasures go and ignore those, now petty, temptations. Just the same there are a great many pleasures to be had and some of them require patience, or even short-term pain, in order to be enjoyed. How do we wisely compare them to immediate, pain-free pleasures?

"It's not hard to make decisions when you know what your values are."
—Roy E. Disney

All of our evaluations of future pleasures require that we use our imagination, and using imagination well is a skill in itself. Learning how to use imagination effectively is what opens the door to an effective pleasure strategy.

We can divide imagination into two types. One type happens when we look at the proposed situation as though it were a picture or a movie. We may or may not see ourselves in that picture; the important feature is that we are looking at the scene from the outside. The other way is to picture ourselves in the scene, experiencing all that is going on firsthand. These are two very different perspectives and affect us differently. Thus, it doesn't make sense to imagine a beach in the Caribbean and seeing my tanning body lying there on a towel (viewing a movie) and then trying to compare that to the yummy feeling of being in a hot tub in the mountains (seeing *and* feeling the experience firsthand). We generally want to compare scenes of the same type, picture or firsthand, in order to judge fairly. Both types of imagination are effective in their own way, but generally we get more visceral information by experiencing ourselves in the scene.

Another part of this skill is dealing with compound imaginary scenes, that is, ones that have both pain and pleasure, possibly separated by time. This is naturally a little trickier than simply one pleasure compared to another. Making things even trickier still is taking into account how much we mind having some pain and how much the pleasure means to us in the moment. As an example, suppose I were to be thinking about a trip to Rio for Carnival. I would at least have to take into account the pain of flying all the way to Brazil and back, the fun of seeing the great spectacle, the undoubted turn-on of sexy bodies on the beach, eating some wonderful food, and the eventual pain of paying off my credit cards. Taking this mixture of visions and feelings and comparing it to the mixture of visions and feelings I might have surrounding staying home and fixing my house requires a lot of work on my part.

But, of course, we do this all the time when we make choices about our futures.

What I hope is useful here is that using pleasure in our decision-making is a multi-stage process. First, we evaluate each scenario on the basis of its total pleasure value, including the feeling of the importance of doing it in our lives. Then, we can compare scenarios on the basis of their relative potential sum-total pleasures. And finally we look to see if we like the result of this evaluation or not.

This is not far from the typical strategy of weighing options for relative benefits. The difference here is that feelings take center stage. No amount of increased benefits will make up for a decision that just doesn't feel good. It doesn't matter how good the travel package is if you really don't want to go there.

I find that sometimes I will go through a process like this and find that I feel the need to choose the option that didn't come out on top. I usually discover some other factor that I had totally overlooked that changes everything. Or sometimes I simply have some intuition that runs contrary to my calculations. But at least, I have made the decision based on both my feelings and my thoughts in a way that took everything into account and with the intention to maximize my joy.

> "However beautiful the strategy, you should occasionally
> look at the results."
> —Winston Churchill

PRESENT PLEASURE OR FUTURE PLEASURE?

Every day we make choices about whether to take a pleasure now or wait. Sometimes the decision is based on the potential for the future pleasure to be greater if we will only be patient. Sometimes we want to save the pleasure to reward ourselves for doing something less pleasurable first. And sometimes we base the decision on the strength of our desire in the present moment allowing the future to take care of itself. Over half of the world's population belongs to religions that promulgate ideas that a life properly led on Earth will yield an afterlife of enormous pleasure (Christianity—2.2 billion, Islam—1.5 billion). The various sects of those religions vary in their definitions of a life properly led, but all of them involve some sacrifice of present pleasure for a much greater pleasure to come.

Some other common choices involve sacrificing present pleasure for future pleasure: working hard in school so that we can get a good job, working hard in a job in order to insure that we can have a good retirement, dieting so that we can have a more pleasing body shape, and working hard to plant a tree for future shade. These examples are obvious, but are they good choices? Does everyone need a good education, as defined by society? Is working for someone else a good choice for everyone? Have we defined "a pleasing body shape" too narrowly? Is our current life expectancy too short to enjoy the future shade? The point I'm making here is that standard notions of what's good/right/appropriate and what's not are no substitute for the skill of feeling into one's own pleasure and making decisions based on that self-knowledge.

This is related to the decisions we have to make regarding those choices that involve both pleasure and pain. For instance, any athlete has to accept that there likely will be some pain involved in becoming good at what they do. Choosing to have a baby carries the same kind of decisions about both pleasure and pain. So does starting a business.

"The doors we open and close each day decide the lives we live."
—Flora Whittemore

One of the trickiest parts of this discussion is present pleasure that has the potential for likely future pain. In other words, are we paying attention to the consequences of our actions, and are we willing to pay the price in the future? We may go ahead and decide to get drunk even though we know we'll have a painful hangover the next morning. Or we may decide to forgo sex because we do not want the risk of contracting something nasty. It can be very hard to judge the consequences of a particular action if we don't have any experience in that realm. That's when we rely on someone we trust to give us a heads up about the possible effects of what we want to do. But we still have the responsibility to evaluate for ourselves the potential pleasure vs. pain consequences in anything we do.

"When it comes to the future, there are three kinds of people:
those who let it happen, those who make it happen,
and those who wonder what happened."
—John M. Richardson, Jr.

While working with the vision of future pleasures can be pleasurable itself, it isn't the same as actually enjoying something. Taking the time to savor something, to wallow in the joy of something is a life-affirming, soul-satisfying activity that nurtures us to our core. But those times often need to be set up, to be organized, perhaps paid for, and certainly, have enough time allotted for their enjoyment. In building a pleasure strategy we need to pay attention to how often we spend an inordinate amount of time working for a specific pleasure without leaving enough time and energy to thoroughly enjoy it. This happens in jobs where the intention is to make enough money to enjoy a good life, but somehow the jobs and the energy it takes to support those jobs soak up almost all of the available time. While there are obvious pleasures in doing work that is useful and effective, there are other facets of our being that want and need to be nurtured by pleasure, too!

"The best thing about the future is that it comes one day at a time."
—Abraham Lincoln

DOES THIS REALLY WORK FOR ME?

I call Developing a Pleasure Strategy a skill because it is something that we can usefully do on a regular basis and we can get better at it the more we do it. It is simply a matter of scanning our lives from time to time and asking, "Does this work for me?" or "Where's the pleasure here?" We don't drive a car down the road in a straight line. We don't sit in one place for a long time without shifting some (unless, perhaps, we're meditating.) We're constantly making adjustments, adjustments that hopefully improve our wellbeing.

Taking the time to check in with ourselves and question what we are doing is like a businessperson reviewing the balance sheet and the profit and loss statement. We won't know where we are if we don't. If we are serious about being happy, we need to have some idea of whether or not we are really doing what it takes.

If we find that we aren't spending the time or energy on the things we care about the most then the solution, at least in the abstract, is obvious. We allocate more time to what we care most about and less to the less important things. However, sometimes we find that it's not so obvious why our pleasure strategy isn't working. Usually, though, we can find the answer in the template we're using—the rules of our personal reality.

The first place to look in this troubleshooting is in permission: is there some way that we are withholding permission? We looked at four questions in Chapter 5 and reviewing them may be helpful.

Another potential source of frustration is a sense that we are trapped in a situation that is unpleasant (or worse) and we can only see feeling good down the road when the situation has changed dramatically. As we've seen before, postponing pleasure without some promise of a reward for doing so is pleasure lost. *There is always something here and now to find joy in.* By focusing on something, anything, that is pleasurable, things start changing. We can always do little things each day that build towards what we truly desire.

> *"Joy is a net of love by which you can catch souls."*
> —Mother Teresa

Building a pleasure strategy that encompasses the full range of our experiences is a big job. But it doesn't have to be done all at once.

Simply taking the time to look up from our busy lives and checking in with ourselves makes a huge difference in how much we can enjoy in this brief time on Earth.

❖ PRACTICING SKILL # 7: ❖
I MAXIMIZE MY PLEASURE BY BEING AWARE OF WHAT IS MOST IMPORTANT TO ME.

Here is a little worksheet to help you sort out all the things that are important to you in one go. This worksheet cannot possibly list every pleasure of every person, so there is room at the bottom to insert your own particular pleasures that aren't listed. This is a very subjective process and you are invited to personalize it in any way that works for you. Just remember that you are trying to find out how effective your personal pleasure strategy is working right now, and, if needed, what areas need more attention.

A PERSONAL PLEASURE STRATEGY WORKSHEET

You are given 100 dollars' worth of evaluation currency. We'll call them "importance dollars." Go down the list and give a dollar to each area of pleasure that is important to you in column A. Then give another dollar in column B to each area that is at least twice as important as the ones you gave a single dollar to in column A. Then give a third dollar in column C to each area that is even more important to you than those with just two dollars. Keep adding dollars to those areas that are more important than the others until you pretty much use up all your "importance dollars." You should have a few pleasures at the end that are clearly more important than all the rest.

Then estimate the hours per week that you typically spend with each of these things you feel are very important to you. This is really a measure of how much personal energy you put into these things, so let the hours reflect your energy devoted to what is important to you. Some things can happen concurrently with others so you can end up with more than a total of 168 hours.

And finally, rate your level of satisfaction with the time you spend on those things you say are important. Use a scale of 0 to 4, where 0 is totally dissatisfied, 1 is somewhat dissatisfied, 2 is pretty neutral, 3 is somewhat satisfied, and 4 is totally satisfied. If you feel the need for more gradations feel free to use decimals.

	A	B	C	D	E	F	G	Hours spent/ week	Satisfaction level
Accomplishment	—	—	—	—	—	—	—	———	———
Order & cleanliness	—	—	—	—	—	—	—	———	———
Romantic love	—	—	—	—	—	—	—	———	———
Friendship	—	—	—	—	—	—	—	———	———
Tastes and smells	—	—	—	—	—	—	—	———	———
Music	—	—	—	—	—	—	—	———	———
Sex	—	—	—	—	—	—	—	———	———
Receive massage/ touch	—	—	—	—	—	—	—	———	———
Learning	—	—	—	—	—	—	—	———	———
Problem solving	—	—	—	—	—	—	—	———	———
Spiritual awareness	—	—	—	—	—	—	—	———	———
Hobbies and games	—	—	—	—	—	—	—	———	———
Beautiful things	—	—	—	—	—	—	—	———	———
Contemplation/ meditation	—	—	—	—	—	—	—	———	———
Exercise/yoga/dance	—	—	—	—	—	—	—	———	———
Service to others	—	—	—	—	—	—	—	———	———
Memories/ memorabilia	—	—	—	—	—	—	—	———	———
Living now in a way that you expect will produce a happy afterlife	—	—	—	—	—	—	—	———	———
Working hard now for a happy retirement	—	—	—	—	—	—	—	———	———
Pleasing other people	—	—	—	—	—	—	—	———	———
Being "right"	—	—	—	—	—	—	—	———	———
Being "righteous"	—	—	—	—	—	—	—	———	———
Being "cool"	—	—	—	—	—	—	—	———	———
Connecting with nature	—	—	—	—	—	—	—	———	———
Risk-taking activities	—	—	—	—	—	—	—	———	———

Exploring physical and/or emotional intensity	—	—	—	—	—	—	—	——	——
Gambling	—	—	—	—	—	—	—	——	——
Devotional activities	—	—	—	—	—	—	—	——	——
Connecting with specific animals (e.g. pets, horses, etc.)	—	—	—	—	—	—	—	——	——
Purely social activities	—	—	—	—	—	—	—	——	——
Media entertainment (television, movies, shows, reading, news)	—	—	—	—	—	—	—	——	——
Family time	—	—	—	—	—	—	—	——	——
Working to take care of others (i.e. a job for the sake of feeding the family)	—	—	—	—	—	—	—	——	——
Lying in the sun	—	—	—	—	—	—	—	——	——
Others	—	—	—	—	—	—	—	——	——

Using the same scale, what is your overall level of satisfaction with the time and energy you spend on the things that you say are important to you? _____

What do you think you will do with this information?_____

_____

NOTE: A downloadable pdf version of this worksheet, which you can then print out and write on, is available at:

http://www.stewartblackburn.com/the-skills-of-pleasure/index.html

The most important thing is to remember the most important thing."
—Anonymous Zen Monk

These are The Skills of Pleasure. They are powerful skills that reward the time and energy for their mastery a hundred fold. They also lead us into a greater awareness of our own being. In the next chapter we move into what we can do with our pleasure beyond simply feeling fabulous. Pleasure is not only the experience of being aligned with our greater being, it is also the energetic platform from which we can shape the experiences that come next.

SECTION III

THE POWER OF PLEASURE

Most of us regard pleasure as the goal and reward for all we do, and quite naturally so. But there is more; being in a state of joy or love is the most powerful place from which we can create, heal, or connect with the divine. It is also how we discover who we are.

"Everything in the universe is with you. Ask all from yourself."
—Rumi

CHAPTER 11

Creating with Pleasure

"Too often we underestimate the power of a touch, a smile, a kind word, a listening ear, an honest compliment, or the smallest act of caring, all of which have the potential to turn a life around."

—Leo F. Buscaglia

We come now to the part where all of the skills we've been practicing come together. We are feeling good, perhaps feeling better than we have ever felt before. And that's just wonderful all by itself. There need not be anything else. But there's even more to pleasure than that. Pleasure has great power. To be more accurate, we are more powerful when we feel good. And we are much more powerful when we feel truly great.

So what does this power look like and what do we do with all this power? In this chapter we will take a look at some of the ways that pleasure is powerful. The first is that it leads us into those realms of consciousness where we can interface with the Higher Mind. It is with the Higher Mind that we experience things like intuition, inspiration, and "knowing." Pleasure shows us the way to that connection and is the prerequisite to the communication that we are looking for.

The second place where we see the power of pleasure is in bringing into our lives that which we desire. This is manifestation and it is what we try to accomplish every day of our lives. We spend most of our days working at changing our personal reality in creative ways by adding or subtracting things, people, ideas, beliefs, feelings, memories, and dreams in such ways that we hope the end results will please us more. I am manifesting a mop if I go to the store and buy myself one. It's too mundane to make any big deal out it. But, if I want a new car and I don't think I can afford one, then "manifesting" a new car is a very big deal.

The third place where we use the power of pleasure is in healing. One might say that this is a particular form of manifestation; after all, we are simply "manifesting" good health. However, it is such an essential part of life that I think it deserves its own category. Pleasure by itself has the power to heal, but it also energizes the efforts we make to come back into harmony with ourselves.

PLEASURE AND THE HIGHER MIND

"Who would then deny that when I am sipping tea in my tearoom I am swallowing the whole universe with it and that this very moment of my lifting the bowl to my lips is eternity itself transcending time and space?"
—D.T. Suzuki

One of the most basic endeavors in all of the world's spiritual systems is that of communicating with the transcendent, be it a god, spirit, ancestor, etc. As I said in the Introduction, this is an experience that most people have had in some way and most would like to have more of. There have been an extraordinary number of techniques developed to access this state of consciousness, ranging from abstinence to Zen. Some of these methods employ drugs of some sort; others use great challenges to the body. Some require long training, while others can be had quite easily.

What unites all of these techniques is two-fold. The primary motivation is to feel amazingly good. We may view it from the perspective of accessing the Sacred or some form of worship. But underneath the details of form, it feels great and we want much more of that. The second similarity in all of these techniques is that access to this consciousness requires relaxation and feeling good to begin with. Now, of course, there are other factors involved: like great focus, a willingness to surrender in some form to the experience, and a letting go of analysis for the time being. But the basics are pretty much the same for all of them.

The methods that use the physical senses, like chanting or singing (as in mantras and hymns), dancing, pictures and artwork (both of divinities and of symbols), spiritual massage, aromas and incense, and foods (both symbolic and delectable), rely on using the feelings engendered by the senses and expanding the awareness beyond the body. Other methods that use only the mind, like meditation, hypnosis, shamanic journeying, and prayer, go from a place of relaxation and feeling good into a greater sense of expansion and peace. In any of these techniques, we relax the thoughts we have about our lives and open to that which is "greater" than the identities that we usually hang on to.

However we arrive at that place, it is the mind in harmony that is open to the messages from within. It doesn't matter who or what we address. The important thing is to ask—ask for help, guidance, inspiration, or whatever we think we are missing in our lives. Once the connection is consciously made, the flow of information and love is open.

Most people's attention to this Higher Mind is about how it can be known in the conscious mind. What is often overlooked is how it feels to be connected to Higher Mind. Frankly, it feels beyond spectacular! It is that wonderful feeling that lets us know that we are connected to Higher Mind.

When we allow ourselves to savor the feelings of that connection, it becomes easy to become completely intoxicated. These feelings are simply and intensely irresistible. It's no wonder that mystics want to spend so much of their time in this magnificent state of being. Everything falls away and only the experience of oneness remains.

"It's de-reamy. It's de-rowsy. It's de-reverie. It's de-rhapsody.
It's de-regal. It's de-royal. It's de-Ritz. It's de-lovely."
—Cole Porter

Now it's hard to get anything else done in this state, and if we are one with All-That-Is, then with whom are we going to party? Cosmic ecstasy is but one of many wonderful feelings. We may want to experience it often, perhaps daily. But we live in a world with lots of other desires flowing around us. Staying healthy is one. Taking care of loved ones is another. Sharing with our community may be one more. When we pay attention, when we feel into it, we can see that all these other ways of being are also connected to our Higher Mind. They all feel wonderful. There is a great pleasure connected to all these things.

In contrast, when we are doing things out of duty or fear, we don't get these great feelings. With duty, we may get a modestly good feeling that we are doing what we are "supposed" to be doing. But I doubt that anyone would ever mistake it for joy.

The Power of Pleasure is the power that comes from our connection to all of who we are. It is like the hum of a well-tuned car or the aroma of a perfectly cooked dish. It is the signal that everything is working as it should. When we are experiencing pleasure we have reduced our resistances and we can then let the inspiration and intuition flow freely. Joy-based decision-making, or pleasure-based thinking is the conscious mind working in partnership with the Higher Mind. It is a collaboration of the highest order.

SEEING THE POWER OF PLEASURE

This fun little exercise requires 5 people and an ordinary chair. One person sits in the chair and the other four get a grip on the chair by the legs. The four lift the chair up a couple of feet into the air, hold it there briefly, and then return the chair to the floor. Let each of the four mentally note the degree of effort in lifting the chair.

Now have each of the four think about someone they really enjoy being with. Let those wonderful feelings pervade their whole bodies.

The four, then, lift the chair up, hold it, and bring it back down. Again, have them note the degree of effort. It's very likely that lifting the chair the second time was a great deal easier than the first time.

PLEASURE AND THE MANIFESTATION PROCESS

Let's look for a moment at how effective we are when we feel good versus when we don't on several different levels.

On a purely physical level, I think it's obvious that when we feel good we get a lot more done. We have more energy, our creativity is higher, our memory is better, and we feel less exhausted at the end of the day. Our whole system works better in general when we are feeling good. This alone should be enough reason to focus on making sure that what we are doing is pleasurable and enjoyable.

But there's more to the power of pleasure than that. As we use our imagination to visualize what we want to do, have, or be next, we are focusing our energy on that new experience. That focus is a big part of the manifestation process: how we bring into our reality the things that we want. For many people the manifestation process is working hard to earn enough money to buy what they need and want. For others the process involves doing things for others who have money so that they will share some of it. And for others still, it involves being clear about what they want, energizing that desire, and letting the universe bring it to them somehow.

All of these methods have one thing in common: they require a strong, energized sense of desire. They *really* want something. As we discussed in the section on desire (Chapter 3), when desire is strong, things happen faster. And the thing that makes desire strong is how good we feel at the thought of fulfilling that desire. It is the feeling of pleasure in the anticipation that fuels that desire and the whole manifestation process.

"By believing passionately in something that still does not exist, we create it. The nonexistent is whatever we have not sufficiently desired."
—Franz Kafka

We do have to act in some fashion to keep things moving in our direction. We can't just enthusiastically desire something and then sit on the couch waiting for it to arrive. We are shaping our reality with our desires, not ordering out for a new one. The desire is a way of focusing our energies; we then need to use our energies to get the job at hand done.

So, when we are feeling the strength of our desire, we are using the anticipated pleasure as a basic tool. Like the lever, the pulley, or the inclined plane, we are willing to go a further distance in order to move something that has a lot of weight. By holding our focus for a while on feeling good and the pleasure of anticipation, we shift the energies around what it is that we are trying to manifest.

Another model is that of the template. Did you ever marvel at how the body always seems to remember how things naturally go back in place when we break a bone or get a cut? Sometimes the body can't quite get things fully back to the template, as in bones that heal crooked. But, for the most part they come back as they're supposed to. In the same way, we have a template of our being, composed of DNA patterns, habits, expectations, hopes and desires, and things that might be called destiny, karma, or calls from our spirit. One of the cool things about this template is that it is malleable. It can be influenced to change. There are plenty of mystical explanations for this phenomenon, like the power of prayer, ritual, or sacrifice. But the main point is that while "reality" may seem objectively fixed, there are thousands of "miracles" that suggest it is not. Even the new understanding that consciousness is a factor in quantum mechanics, gives us permission to assume that our desires matter in the workings of our template.

"I was exhilarated by the new realization that I could change the character of my life by changing my beliefs. I was instantly energized because I realized that there was a science-based path that would take me from my job as a perennial "victim" to my new position as 'co-creator' of my destiny."

—Bruce H. Lipton

What, then, are the mechanisms for changing the template? In essence, how do we change the patterns that form the basis of our reality?

The template is with us at all times. That means that it is a non-physical aspect of our self, just like our conscious mind, our sub-conscious, and our Higher Mind. This template is the ordering of our personal world. All the aspects of us refer to it as we go about constructing each new moment. It is generally considered to be a part of the subconscious and held in memory.

As we have noted before, one of the things about memory, which is notoriously flexible and selective, is that the strongest memories have the most energetic feelings attached to them. We remember the things that upset us, that hurt us, that made us feel especially proud, that we got very excited about, or that were especially important to us.

When we want to change our template we want to do it in a way that we'll remember. Therefore, we have to give the new template energy or importance to make it stick. And the best source of that energy is pleasure.

This is why when we envision something we want to do, be, or have, we want to feel as though it is taking place right now. We are changing the template in this moment and we want to make sure that our subconscious gets it. But what is often overlooked in this process is that the subconscious will only make it important enough to override previous orders if the new orders have more energy than the old ones. Thus, we need to feel the great pleasure of the new orders. The visualizing process needs to include as much envisioned pleasure as possible. And that means getting excited, delighted, and filled with great joy. This is where the power of savoring is so valuable. The more intensely we can savor, the more energy we are giving to our new template piece.

Or we can use the magic of gratitude.

GRATITUDE AND CREATION

Gratitude is a very curious phenomenon and we've discussed it some previously. It is very useful when pleasures come to an end.

We recognize that we have enjoyed something that didn't have to happen, but it did. We honor the happy memories. And we acknowledge all that went in to the event we so liked. Our "thank you" sums it all up and then we are ready to go on to the next wonderful experience.

But gratitude can be used in other powerful ways. We can use gratitude to help us manifest what it is that we desire. When we summon the feeling of gratitude for something that has not yet appeared to us, we are reinforcing the new orders in our template. We tend to think of gratitude as being about something that has already happened. But it isn't restricted to that use.

> *"Gratitude unlocks the fullness of life. It turns what we have into enough, and more. It turns denial into acceptance, chaos to order, confusion to clarity. It can turn a meal into a feast, a house into a home, a stranger into a friend."*
>
> —Melody Beattie

Gratitude is a focusing on something we feel good about. It may be a memory that inspires this gratitude or it may be something in our active experience. Either way it is always something that we feel positive about. If we didn't actually like it we wouldn't be grateful. So when we bring gratitude into the scene we are already feeling good about something. And by being grateful for something in our template we are expressing our current joy about its presence right now and thus energizing it. And the gratitude keeps us in the present, where our power to change things is.

In terms of our outer life, this means envisioning something that we want and then being grateful for it as though it has already happened. But in terms of our inner life, we are simply being grateful for the change in our life, essentially a new us. We are somewhat different in that the change in our template changes our experience of both the world outside and our world inside.

Pleasure and Healing

*"Eventually you will come to understand that love heals everything,
and love is all there is."*

—Gary Zukov

One of the most important desires for manifestation revolves around healing, both for ourselves and for others. But, before we discuss how we can use pleasure for healing, let's look at what healing is.

It has long been acknowledged in scientific circles that stress is related to illness, though the connection isn't always clear. What is clear is that stress in the body releases hormones that put the muscles of the body in a defensive mode. They tighten up.

When we have thoughts about things we don't want to do, many muscles also tighten up. In fact, anything that we find unpleasant causes us to tighten our muscles. And when we tighten up our muscles chronically, we constrict the flow of bodily fluids like blood and lymph. Emotionally, we reduce the awareness of unpleasant feelings when we tighten up as well. This is, of course, how most of us cope with the difficult feelings we encounter in daily life.

Unfortunately, when too many feelings are being resisted, we block serious amounts of fluids and energy from flowing in the natural, healthy way they were meant to flow. Most scientists and doctors would suggest that this stress causes us to be less resistant to germs and disease vectors and makes us more vulnerable to these problems. It is at this stage that doctors then intervene and use their own particular forms of magic to alleviate pain and cure diseases.

One of the most useful ways of looking at stress is from the perspective of feelings. If we have two thoughts that each evoke a strong desire, and those two desires are in conflict, then the emotional body is being pulled in two directions and we have stress. If, for example, I want to go to the movies but my spouse wants to stay home and play cards with me, then I may well be mildly torn between my desire to see the movie and my desire to please my spouse. On a larger scale, if I have no money in my bank account and I want to feed my children, but I don't want to commit a crime in order to do so, then I have a more powerful clash of desires. Or if I have a desire to have sexual relations with someone, but I also desire to not let it be known that I have those desires for fear of substantial repercussions, then I set myself up for serious conflict. This is all fairly obvious.

> *"The greatest weapon against stress is our ability to choose*
> *one thought over another."*
> —William James

What is not so obvious is that all of this stress was created in my mind with my thoughts. My thoughts flowed from my desires, and the feelings that came from those conflicting thoughts created stress. I can feel that stress even more strongly than the desires and something has to give. I may say that being with my spouse is more important to me than the movies and resolve the conflict that way. I may allow my children to go hungry for a while until I can get some money because I am adamant about not breaking the law (or resolve the situation in the opposite way.) And I may repress my sexual desires because they might lead to an intolerable situation. In each case I make a choice that minimizes the conflict of ideas in my head.

However, if I am often in conflict and am creating stress, then my life becomes dominated by the stress. My thoughts may regularly be ones like: my spouse never pays attention to what I want to do and what my needs are and I don't like that. Or, I never have enough money to feed the family and I hate that. Or, I cry a lot because I don't know what to do with these sexual feelings that I can't safely express.

We can see that stress like we see in these little vignettes, is an important factor in disease and illness. When that stress is relieved generally the symptoms disappear rapidly. If we've been living with the stress for a long time, we may well not know where the stress came from. But when we can find the stress and relieve it, miracles can occur. I see this frequently in the work I do. Find a different way to think about the stressing factors, thus reducing the overall stress, and the symptoms begin to clear up.

"We must have a pie. Stress cannot exist in the presence of a pie."
—David Mamet

There are some caveats to this. Sometimes a person doesn't really want to fully heal. The physical problem may serve them in some way, as in providing an income through disability payments. Or they may receive kind attention that would otherwise be absent. We are always trying to maximize feeling good and the ways that other people choose to do that may be different from our own.

There may be multiple stressors and getting rid of, or at least reducing, one or two, may not go far enough. And for some people changing to a new way of being, i.e., healthier, may be more of a stress than the illness. But for those who are ready and willing to change how they think and feel, this kind of healing is often very effective. It is based on finding new thoughts and feelings that don't produce conflict and, in fact, are supportive of positive feelings about oneself.

I have dealt with numerous people who have shown remarkable results simply by changing their thinking. Many healers can tell similar stories. More important than these anecdotal stories are your own personal experiments. When you get sick next, see if you can find the emotional component. It is likely to be some kind of stress that your body is trying to relieve.

I'm not suggesting that germs and accidents aren't genuine factors as well. But it is remarkable how quickly we return to good health when we change our situation from one of stress, as in "I hate my job (or relationship, living place, life situation, etc.)" into one of joy, or love, or fun. When we actively choose pleasure, the world around us changes.

HEALING OURSELVES

One of the most useful assumptions is that my body is always working for my general welfare. We may not recognize what it's doing or why, but if I assume that my body is always trying to solve a problem, then I can more easily see what I can do to assist it. For instance, if I catch a cold and find that I need to stay in bed for a few days, I have several ways of looking at it. If I assume that I have "caught" a cold from some random donor, then I am constrained to just sit out the cold as best I can. If I assume that the cold is some punishment for something I did, like sitting in a draft or getting my feet wet, then I suffer whatever is appropriate. Or if I assume that my body "chose," for its own reasons, to force me into some rest for my overall health or to relieve some particular stress, then I am empowered to make the most of my rest and, perhaps, learn other ways of relieving my stress.

> "We casually assume that a person who survives cancer or can cure himself of a fatal disease operates with the same mental machinery as anyone else, but this is not true: mental processes can be deep or shallow. To go deep means to contact the hidden blueprint of intelligence and change it—only then can visualization of fighting cancer, for example, be strong enough to defeat the disease."
>
> —Deepak Chopra

To think that our bodies don't know what they're doing is to invite battles, big and small, between our conscious mind and our body-mind. This lack of respect is like telling our car mechanic how to do his job. Very dangerous! Keep the body happy (and the mechanic) and we maximize the team effort and our general effectiveness.

The whole premise here is that when we are feeling good we return to health quickly and easily. When we fight ourselves, we create unnecessary pain. The key is to pay attention to how we are feeling and to make the choices necessary to feel good again.

In our efforts to feel better, sometimes we go looking for things to heal, like suppressed problems, personal demons, or long-lost soul pieces. This is done with the assumption that once found and healed we will feel better. If we don't change our beliefs and attitudes, though, we will likely recreate those very problems we wanted to fix.

On the other hand, when we start by intentionally doing everything we can to feel better, anything that inhibits that better feeling comes up and can be dealt with more easily. The things that need healing will appear and anything that doesn't appear probably doesn't need our conscious help. Pleasure heals by itself.

DISTANCE HEALING, DISTANT JOY

When we want something for someone else, like better health, better emotional wellbeing, problems resolved, we are getting involved with distant healing. Most religions and spiritual systems have some form for doing this. Prayer has always been a common one. In other times sacrifice was sometimes done. Nowadays we send a card, an email, or text message conveying our wish that they feel better. All of these start with a desire on our part: we want, for ourselves, for them to feel better. To my mind, there's nothing wrong with selfishly wanting someone else to feel better. We don't like being aware of their suffering and, perhaps, we empathetically feel what they're feeling.

> *"The greatest healing therapy is friendship and love."*
> —Hubert H. Humphrey

It's quite natural to want to do something and very often the only thing we can do is to send them some distant healing. However, what we want to send them are feelings of pleasure and joy, not the feelings of pity, sorrow, or fear. What we are feeling at the time of our prayer or intent is what we are sending. Misery may like company, but not for long.

So when we are thinking about someone who needs some kind of healing, it is important to be aware of what we are sending. The thoughts that we have about how we would like their lives to be different aren't nearly as powerful as the feelings that go with them. Essentially, we are working with the greater template of life. We are looking to influence, in our own way, the realities of other people. They, of course, have their own free will and may decide for their own reasons not to accept our desire for some change in them. Whatever is going on may be serving them in ways that we have no idea about. But we can offer our feelings to them, and if they choose to accept, they can use the energy of those feelings any way they like.

I feel awkward here talking about how this works because the best we can do is offer models and theories. There is enough evidence, mostly circumstantial but by no means all, that this kind of thing does work. People like to understand the mechanics of how things work and many, many meanings have been created to explain this. I suggest you find one you like and feel good about and allow that one to be your truth. For myself, I prefer to simply say that this stuff works and I let it go at that.

"I'm touched by the idea that when we do things that are useful and helpful—collecting these shards of spirituality—that we may be helping to bring about a healing."
—Leonard Nimoy

One of the things that works better than any other I know is to make sure that we are feeling the way we want others to feel when we send them our good wishes. That means getting into as wonderful a state as we possibly can beforehand. We focus on our own happiness, and then invite others into it.

One of the side benefits of wishing others well is the fabulous feelings we get to enjoy. We offer a certain vibration to them and the stronger we make that vibration the more effective it seems to be. This is the operating principle of many holy people who spend large amounts of time sending love around the world. It's a fine practice to do, if it appeals to you.

❖ THE CHOCOLATE HEALING ❖

Here is a fun healing technique that works often enough to keep in our personal medicine bag. It is very useful if you have either a physical pain or an emotional pain that you can locate the place in the body where you feel it most. This is a derivative of Serge Kahili King's Dynamind Technique where we use chocolate instead of tapping or humming. Feel into the part of the body where you notice the pain and find a way to rate the level of intensity of the pain. A scale from zero to ten works well, with zero being no pain at all and ten being unbelievably bad pain.

Start by taking a bite-sized piece of a chocolate that you particularly like and eat half that piece. Put as much attention as you can on enjoying the chocolate. Let yourself enjoy it all the way down to your toes. Now say the works, "I have a pain in my_____. And that can change. I want that pain to go away." Put the other piece of chocolate in your mouth and enjoy that until the pleasure fades away. Now go back and check the level of intensity of the pain and see if there has been a change. Repeat as often as necessary, or until you've run out of chocolate!

Now that we've crafted our lives to our liking, it's time to put the finishing touches on. It's like making the perfect banana split. We've peeled the nice, ripe banana and sliced it lengthwise. We've put three big scoops of our favorite ice cream on top of the banana. We've poured chocolate syrup over the ice cream. We've piped whipped cream all around the edges, and sprinkled lots of little bits of candy or nuts everywhere. It's now time to put the cherry on top!

CHAPTER 12

The Cherry on Top

*I searched for God, and found only myself. I searched for myself,
and found only God."*

—Sufi Proverb

We've come a long way through the Principles and Skills of
Pleasure. We have looked at some foundational ideas: that pleasure is only experienced in the present, that we have the choice as to
how we feel, and that pleasure shows us how connected we are to our
core self. We have explored the skills of awareness, permission, adventure, choosing, savoring, letting go, and creating a strategy. We have
even examined using pleasure for healing, manifesting, and intuition.

But, perhaps the greatest magic that pleasure has is in showing us
who we are. The more we pay attention to how we are feeling the more
we get to know ourselves. Rather than relying on the theories and concepts of others, we discover for ourselves what works and what doesn't.
It is in knowing ourselves that we find the greatest pleasures of all.

In this final chapter we will explore some of life's truly great feelings, the ones that people fight for, sacrifice for, build religions and civ-
ilizations around, and sometimes come to know intimately in ecstasy

and bliss. Most connoisseurs of great feelings seem to concur that the greatest feelings arise when we are totally connected to our core, Higher Mind, or All-That-Is. This magnificent connection to the deepest parts of who we are is what I call the cherry on top of our banana split!

THE PLEASURE OF CONNECTION

*"The connections we make in the course of a life—
maybe that's what heaven is."*
—Fred Rogers

In many ways the pleasure of connection is the fundamental pleasure of life. We feel nurtured and loved through our connections. We get a sense of our own validity; we feel that we matter. When we connect, we open up a little bit and enjoy the delicious freedom in letting down our defenses.

What is particularly interesting, though, is that it really doesn't matter what we connect to. We can feel that pleasure when we connect to our family, familiar animals, our concept of divinity, the earth, our sports team, our car, or our favorite chair. For many people, their connections to the place they live, their communities, and their lifestyle comprise the foundation for their happiness. For others, the connections to specific people fulfill that need. But what is true for all of them is that the deeper the connection, the greater the potential for pleasure.

A real connection isn't a conceptual thing; it is an awareness of feeling. We feel connection. We feel a kind of relatedness, a sense of communality. At a deeper level, it is recognition that we are all parts of the same spiritual family. This awareness, fleeting as it sometimes is, allows us to see into ourselves a little bit, into some facets of who we are. And that experience almost always feels good.

There are some cultures that prize connection and the feelings that go with that above all else. This is particularly true of the Hawaiians with their ethic of Aloha, a loving relationship to all things and beings. Many other indigenous societies place a similar value on connection. But in most modern cultures, connection in everyday life takes a back seat to more "important" things, like getting things done and "taking care of business." The pleasure of connection is so overlooked that many wouldn't recognize it as a major pleasure. I know I didn't for a great many years. Once I became aware of what I was missing, I let go of a lot of other efforts to find pleasure. They simply didn't hold a candle to the daily pleasures of connection.

"Of all the things which wisdom provides to make life entirely happy, much the greatest is the possession of friendship."
—Epicurus

So take the time to admire, appreciate, bless, give thanks for, and press the "Like" button. When we put our attention on the things and people we like and feel good about, we strengthen our connection to those things and people. A simple compliment becomes a cord of connection. If fostered, that cord may grow into thick rope that holds us deeply and securely in connection and joy.

Appreciation of any kind feels good to us. It is how we nurture our connections. We can appreciate anything, just so long as it feels real to us. When we silently appreciate something like someone's clothes we both feel better ourselves, and we also feel closer to that person. When we actually vocalize an appreciation, it draws us in like a magnet. Judgmental criticisms, of course, do just the opposite.

"But I'll tell you what hermits realize. If you go off into a far, far forest and get very quiet, you'll come to understand that you're connected with everything."
—Alan Watts

So when we are considering doing something, something that we think will feel good, it can be very useful to remember the pleasure of connection and whether a given action maintains one or more connections or breaks them. Too often we think we are maximizing our pleasure with some activity, but neglect to see if what we are doing is actually diminishing our pleasure by breaking some connection. Lying to get what we want is an example of this. Putting someone down in order to make us feel a little better is another one. We are overlooking the effects of what we are doing and risk losing valuable connections to other people.

A properly functioning pleasure strategy generally takes connection significantly into account. We want to increase the pleasure of our connections and avoid breaking connections to people we care about as much as possible. Getting angry is a natural part of life. Wanting to do something about that anger is also natural. However, when we take the pleasure of connection into account, we may want to modify our response in such a way as to maintain as much connection as we possibly can.

Love, Compassion, and the Pleasure of Helping Others

"Love and compassion are health-skills in which we can train ourselves."
—Dawson Church

One variant of the pleasure of connection is the pleasure of helping others. We need to be around and interact with other people, to a greater or lesser extent. And there is very limited satisfaction to being happy when everyone around us is not. By paying attention to another's happiness we increase the general level of happiness and that raises our own happiness significantly.

I have not spoken of love much in this book because there is so much said about love, and people have such strong but differing ideas about it. However, it is a major experience of life and we all look to it as a cornerstone of our happiness.

Love is a particular form of pleasure. It feels good and we enjoy it. It follows the trajectory of pleasure and, as such, it works the way other pleasures do. But it is distinguished by its being the essence of connection. It is what we experience when we are connected to anything, inside or out.

Compassion is the feeling we get when we see some sort of suffering and we want to do something about it. It is a magnificent feeling and particularly prized by Buddhists, who regard it as the supreme feeling. It is a great motivation for doing whatever we can to help someone else.

> *"If you want others to be happy, practice compassion.*
> *If you want to be happy, practice compassion."*
> —Dalai Lama

As we have said before, pleasure is contagious. People like being around happy people. When we hold our own pleasure and a sense of wellbeing in the midst of chaos and fear, it has a definite calming effect. The strongest emotion generally sets the tone for a group of people. If you can be the strongest in your sense of feeling good, others will resonate with you.

Even in the ordinary duties of everyday life, by choosing pleasure and paying attention to feeling good, other people will respond, as if by magic. A smile will beget a smile; a kind word will beget a heartfelt "thank you." Even waiting until someone answers you when you ask, "How are you?" will have a pronounced effect.

> *"Simple kindness to one's self and to all that lives*
> *is the most transformational force of all."*
> —David Hawkins

A big part of increasing the world's level of wellbeing is letting go of the judgments we carry around about how other people should live their lives. Just as we do not want others to tell us how to live, almost everyone else feels the same way. I find it very profitable to make the assumption that every one of us is doing the best that we know how. Certainly there is plenty of room for learning how to live life more effectively and enjoyably. But there is no reason why we should be expected to know how to do that perfectly right now. We are all learning. To lovingly and kindly assist in someone else's learning is wonderful. To criticize someone is to make them wrong and has the effect of reducing their level of wellbeing. It rarely teaches them anything except how to endure more pain and shame.

The Pleasure of Presence

"And as we let our own light shine, we unconsciously give other people permission to do the same. As we are liberated from our fear, our presence automatically liberates others."

—Marianne Williamson

There is a certain joy that we get when all the madness and chatter disappear and we are left alone with ourselves in the moment. Being present allows us to let go of all of our fears of the future and all the regrets and pains that we might have associated with our past. Being present just leaves us with what is in front of us. It is the joy of being fully aware of the details all around us. In this feeling state we can delight in each little sparkle on a leaf, each curve of a branch, each hue of color in a flower.

When all of the distractions are banished, our awareness can expand and contract at will. It is in this state that we can appreciate curiosity, wonder, and awe. Our own sense of where we fit in becomes fluid and we can go from an awareness of tiny little insects to an amazement at the glory and vastness of the Universe. This is the realm of the poet and we have an open invitation to come in anytime.

There is one very special pleasure of presence: to savor ourselves. This is not something that most of us can do immediately. We have been thoroughly trained to keep our attention on what is going on outside of us. There is a kind of taboo, as Alan Watts put it, on knowing who we are. However, it is in this space of looking into ourselves that we can most powerfully affect our self-esteem.

The key to self-esteem is feeling good about our personal value. And the key to that is to be good with who we are, to know that there is nothing wrong with us. And the key to that is to value our uniqueness.

In our society, we have become obsessed with what is "normal" or "ideal." Neither concept is useful for appreciating our individual features and our own particular contributions to the world. In former times a person was often known by his or her trade, the job they had in a society. Perhaps they didn't have the freedom to change their lives the way we do, but at least they had something that was valued as part of their identity.

The focus on sameness has created a sense of how we are "supposed" to be regardless of how we actually experience ourselves. Rather than helping us to identify ourselves as distinct and distinctive human beings, we have been led to believe that self-value is based on how well we match up to the idea of perfection. That, of course, is a no-win situation; by definition we can never be "perfect." It's a sure-fire path to stress and illness.

We can feel relaxed and peaceful when we accept that we are both different from all others and essentially the same as well. It's a paradox that we can hold like a talisman. It reminds us that we can magically look at things from different perspectives, depending on what our needs are at the moment.

"Today you are You, that is truer than true. There is no one alive who is Youer than you."

—Dr. Seuss

One step beyond appreciating our uniqueness is actively savoring our being. As we explored in Chapter 8, savoring is not only enjoying something, it is enjoying something while excluding any negative thoughts or feelings. It is simply taking the time to fully enjoy what we are focusing on. When we savor ourselves we stay in the space of feeling really good about ourselves. We allow ourselves to just be, without any need of fixing anything, without need of becoming anything more (or less), and without need of anything from the past or the future. We're talking about savoring that goes beyond simple presence. Our focus is on the pleasure being experienced as well as the source of that pleasure.

"At the time of euphoria and expansion caused by delicate foods and drinks, be total in this delight, and through it, taste supreme bliss."

—The Vijnanabhairava Tantra

The mind doesn't need to do much when we savor. However, it does need to have a role or it will get antsy. And it's an important role that it plays. The mind needs to keep the focus on what are we experiencing in this moment. Maintaining that focus allows us to sink into a deep awareness of the pleasure of being. It allows us to be at peace with ourselves and all that we are. We can turn our attention to the things that we aspire to or would like to change later. Now is the moment of simple pleasures. Now is the time to enjoy the present moment and our place in that moment. It is our opportunity to sense our aliveness and to be aware of how good a relaxed breath is.

The Elements of Savoring Yourself

The first element of savoring ourselves is to banish criticism and judgment. We simply look at what we are experiencing and give ourselves permission to enjoy it as it is. The second element is take time for it. Remember that time is pleasure's best friend. And the third is to be aware not only of ourselves as the subject of the savoring, but also to be aware of the experience of enjoying all these aspects of who we are.

You might want to experiment with savoring and enjoying how you love and what you love, your sexuality, your compassion for others, your particular skills, or all of your suppressed hungers and desires. There is no reason not to enjoy all aspects of who you are. Just set aside some time in a quiet place and feel as much as you can of the wonderful but perhaps challenging feelings that are part of your deeper world. This little experiment can be amazingly powerful and wonderful.

One way of describing it is that when you feel really great, the parts of you that don't resonate with that great feeling show themselves and demand to be dealt with. Please don't be alarmed that they come up; they usually can be dealt with by acknowledging them. But be firm that you are now living in such a way that they are no longer relevant or welcome. It's like digging a hole. We may be very happy with a hole we have dug and go to bed pleased with ourselves at how deep we went. But in the morning the hole isn't as deep as it was. The sides have caved in some and there's more debris in the bottom. The overly steep sides had to be dealt with at some point anyway. And the debris in the bottom is pretty easy to get up. So we get back to the wonderful place we found with a little bit more work, knowing that it has become more stable than when we first encountered it.

> *"Do not be satisfied with the stories that come before you.*
> *Unfold your own myth."*
>
> —Rumi

You can always change who you are, at least on the level of personality. One day you may decide that you have been a mother long enough. The kids are grown and your role as caretaker of them is complete. Sure, you may well put some of your energy into supporting their wellbeing. But perhaps it's time now to become someone else: maybe a painter, an activist, or a healer. Or you might decide to become a more successful salesman and, in so deciding, you now fully embrace the role of a *truly successful* salesman. Or perhaps you decide to become a great lover and thus become a master of the sensuous and pleasing.

Each of these new roles involves using your creative energies to craft a new you. We change our experience of the world from inside, by changing who we are in small but significant ways. There is great pleasure in playing with who we are in this moment. The deeper parts of us don't change. We're like both the author and the actors in a play. The author in us stays the same, but we get to play an infinite number of roles. We get to try out parts that intrigue us or give us some adventure to learn from. Some roles we must play for a long time once we choose them; others we can let go of like old shoes. The point is to find the pleasure in these acts of creation and savor ourselves as we fashion each new variation of us.

Where's the Pleasure?

Follow the pleasure. Look for it always. Keep asking the question, "Where's the pleasure here?" It will unerringly lead you to who you are. Each step helps you shape your life, it shows you more about what brings you joy and what doesn't. Keeping the focus on "Where's the pleasure?" can help you move swiftly up the scale of feelings. Another way of doing this process is to ask, "Is what I am doing making me feel good?" or "Does this action really work for me?" This is also an efficient path to wisdom.

This is much more than "Do what thou wilt"; it is about "What are your deepest desires?" and "What do you really want?" This is the Great Adventure of Life—exploring who we are by exploring our greatest pleasures: what makes us excited, happy, and joyful.

❖ SAVORING YOURSELF ❖

How might this look? You might start by enjoying how you are creating yourself at this moment. So savor the creative act of being you today. It is a creation that expresses your soul. The fuller the expression, the better it feels.

Find a place to relax quietly for a while and get very comfortable. Take a few moments to be aware of your unique perspectives and perceptions. These are things like your opinions and beliefs, the things that tickle your funny bone, your sense of style, what a great adventure looks like to you, the colors that perk you up, the activities that give you the most satisfaction, the music you like, your comfort foods, and the people who energize you the most. Let these pleasures fill you up and recognize that these are the things that make you who you are.

Try savoring some of the things you have already created or helped to create. You probably have things that you have done connected to your work that you found satisfying. Think about the ways that you have created a living environment that suites you. Think about the relationships you have enjoyed, the connections you have built, and all the fun times that you have helped to create. As you think about these things, feel the joy connected to them and savor those feelings.

Now allow your thoughts to move to those things that you want to create. You might want to consider the different aspects of your living environment that you would like to change or add. Is there any kind of artistic expression you would like put your energies into? Perhaps you would like to create more wonderful relationships with people, animals, or the earth. Each of these acts of creation is an expression of you. Savor yourself as you prepare to go forth to do them.

You are an expression of All-That-Is and you have the power to enjoy it fully.

May your pleasures be many; may all your dreams be fulfilled; and may your radiant joy illuminate the world.

Made in the USA
San Bernardino, CA
17 October 2013